Scripture

Scripture

History and Interpretation

Dianne Bergant

Tatha Wiley, Series Editor

A Michael Glazier Book

LITURGICAL PRESS
Collegeville, Minnesota

www.litpress.org

A Michael Glazier Book published by Liturgical Press

Cover design by Ann Blattner

Excerpts from documents of the Second Vatican Council are from *Vatican Council II: The Basic Sixteen Documents*, by Austin Flannery, OP © 1996 (Costello Publishing Company, Inc.). Used with permission.

Scripture texts in this work are taken from the *New American Bible with Revised New Testament and Revised Psalms* © 1991, 1986, 1970 Confraternity of Christian Doctrine, Washington, D.C. and are used by permission of the copyright owner. All Rights Reserved. No part of the *New American Bible* may be reproduced in any form without permission in writing from the copyright owner.

1   2   3   4   5   6   7   8   9

Library of Congress Cataloging-in-Publication Data

Bergant, Dianne.
    Scripture : history and interpretation / Dianne Bergant.
        p.   cm. — (Engaging theology: Catholic perspectives)
    "A Michael Glazier book."
    Includes bibliographical references and indexes.
    ISBN 978-0-8146-5995-3
    1. Bible—Criticism, interpretation, etc.   2. Catholic Church—Doctrines.
    I. Title.

    BS511.3.B47   2008
    220.6—dc22

                                                    2007041521

Contents

Editor's Preface

In calling the Second Vatican Council, Pope John XXIII challenged those he gathered to take a bold leap forward. Their boldness would bring a church still reluctant to accept modernity into full dialogue with it. The challenge was not for modernity to account for itself, nor for the church to change its faith, but for the church to transform its conception of faith in order to speak to a new and different situation.

Today we stand in a postmodern world. The assumptions of modernity are steeply challenged, while the features of postmodernity are not yet fully understood. Now another world invites reflection and dialogue, and the challenge is to discover how the meanings and values of Christian faith speak effectively to this new situation.

This series takes up the challenge. Central concerns of the tradition— God, Jesus, Scripture, Anthropology, Church, and Discipleship—here are lifted up. In brief but comprehensive volumes, leading Catholic thinkers lay out these topics with a historically conscious eye and a desire to discern their meaning and value for today.

Designed as a complete set for an introductory course in theology, individual volumes are also appropriate for specialized courses. Engaging Theology responds to the need for teaching resources alive to contemporary scholarly developments, to the current issues in theology, and to the real questions about religious beliefs and values that people raise today.

Tatha Wiley
Series Editor

Introduction

What is an introduction to the Bible? While an introduction does not usually deal with simply the biblical text itself, it does prepare one to read the text with greater understanding and insight. This introduction will be best used if it is read along with the biblical text itself. Most study Bibles include outlines of the text, maps and charts, and other aids that will help in understanding. An introduction itself is not a short version of the longer work. That would be a survey or a synopsis. An introduction is concerned with questions such as: What? Who? Where? When? How? Why?

What?

Just what is the Bible? Some might say that the Bible is the word of God in human words. True—but what does that mean? Is it a collection of rules that sets the direction of our lives? Both biblical testaments do indeed contain laws and regulations, but the Bible itself is not a rulebook. Is it a compilation of teaching that we must accept? Again, there is a great deal of instruction in both biblical testaments, but the Bible is not a catechism. Is it a chronicle of the events in the lives of the people of ancient Israel and of the early Christian era? While there certainly seems to be a historical base to many of the biblical narratives, and the expression "salvation history" has long been a popular way of understanding the movement of those narratives, the Bible is not a book of history. Is it merely an assemblage of the religious literature developed by a particular ancient Near Eastern people, handed down generation after generation until people receive it today? It certainly is religious literature, but we believe that its message was inspired by God and, in a unique way, that it continues to reveal something about God even to us today.

An introduction will help us to understand *what* the Bible is. It will lead us through much of the complexity of this collection of diverse biblical books, explaining why some books were included in the collection and considered inspired by God, and why other books were not. An introduction will help us to identify the religious importance of traditions, practices, and customs that may seem strange to us because they come from a very different culture and age. It will throw light on the meaning of various biblical-theological terms, such as inspiration, revelation, canon, and hermeneutics.

Who?

To say that the Bible is the word of God in human words raises the question of authorship. Who is the author of Scripture? *Dei Verbum* (The Dogmatic Constitution on Divine Revelation), one of the most important documents of the Second Vatican Council (Vatican II), clearly states that "the books of the Old and the New Testaments, whole and entire, with all their parts . . . have God as their author" (11). What does this mean? Did God actually take stylus or quill in hand and write down each word that we consider inspired? Or did God choose certain individuals, inspire them with a divine message, and commission them to do the writing like a stenographer, as earlier religious art often suggests? If God authored the Scriptures in either of these ways, how can the discrepancies found in the Bible be explained? For example, the first account of creation claims that light was created before the sun, the moon, and the stars. How could this be? In the Gospels of Mark, Luke, and Matthew, the adult Jesus goes to Jerusalem only once, the time he was arrested and put to death. However, in John, he travels there several times to celebrate festivals. If God is the author of the Bible, how can there be contradictions in these accounts?

An introduction will address the complicated question of biblical authorship: *who* wrote the Bible? It will show that individuals and groups of believers shaped and reshaped the religious traditions in such a way that, without denying divine involvement in the development of the biblical tradition, these human beings can be considered authentic authors in their own right. In addressing this process, this introduction will also treat the meaning and function of both inspiration and revelation.

Where?

Within the recent past, theologians have come to realize the significance of geography in the development of theology. They view geography not as merely the place where events unfold but as a factor in determining the form that theology takes. For instance, the notion of primordial happiness conceived as a garden (Gen 2:8) would have originated only in a community that enjoyed nourishment from and delight in the fruits of the earth. Towering mountains with the majesty that they possess came to epitomize divine dignity and magnificence to those people who lived in their regal shadow. The life-giving character of running water, so valued by those who knew the cravings of thirst, became an apt analogy of the goodness and grace of God. The parables of Jesus show that he too appreciated the role that geography can play in theology. He compared the reign of God to a field into which seed had been sown, thus appealing to the farmer, or to a net cast into the sea, an image so familiar to the fisherfolk.

An introduction to the Bible will argue that geography is not an insignificant aspect of reality, particularly for people of traditional cultures like those of the ancient Near East. It will show how topography influences economic status, political struggle, national and religious identity. It will provide a sketch of the geographic landscape that played such an important role in shaping the inner landscape of the biblical people. The way they understood their relationship with God was influenced by places *where* they encountered God.

When?

One of the fundamental principles of biblical faith is the conviction that God is present and active in human history. This belief does not originate with the Christian faith. Even a cursory reading of some of the earliest Old Testament stories shows that the ancient Israelites believed that God was in their midst. For example, God spoke to Moses from the burning bush while Moses was tending the flock of Jethro, his father-in-law (Exod 3:4). Similarly, in the New Testament God called Saul as he was on his way to persecute more Christians (Acts 9:1-9). Stories like these lay bare the importance and value of human history, human interests, and human aspirations. They also show that the way we experience God, understand that experience, and speak about it are influenced by the circumstances that hold sway at the time. As with everything historical, biblical stories, directives, and proclamations all reflect the currents of thought, the customs, and the insights of the time. To grasp the meaning of the biblical passage, it is important to appreciate the circumstances of its time of origin.

An introduction to the Bible will note the major historical events that influenced the faith of ancient Israel and that of early Christianity. It will trace the most important historical trajectories that shaped the biblical traditions. Prominent aspects of religious traditions carry the features of the times *when* they were developed. The introduction will examine these features in order to discover the meaning behind them.

How?

The answer to this question depends on one's understanding of authorship. No one can doubt that the word of God in the Bible has come down to us in human words. If God was the only authentic author of these words, then humans were merely instruments in God's hands, inscribing the words that God dictated. This raises the question of inspiration. Were the writers inspired or were the words inspired, or were both inspired? And how did this happen? If the words of Scripture are God's words, how are limited human beings able to understand them? Did God condescend to make some kind of accommodation to human frailty? Did God dictate in the language of the human author? Or are the ideas God's, but the words those of the human author? On the other hand, if the entire community was involved in shaping and reshaping of the biblical tradition, how and where does inspiration enter the picture?

An introduction will explain *how* the biblical traditions developed out of the experience of people who believed that God was present in their midst, calling them forward into lives in union with that God, guiding them as they struggled through the unknown reality of life, protecting them as they faced challenges and dangers, and forgiving them when they were unfaithful to their identity as God's own people. It will demonstrate how these traditions survived as they were reinterpreted in new situations for new generations facing new challenges. It will explain the role of inspiration throughout this entire process.

Why?

This question can be answered in various ways. First and most obviously, the ancient Israelites and the early Christians developed and handed down their religious traditions because that is what people do. They tell their stories; they proclaim their values; they decide on their customs; and they pass these on to the next generation as that generation is socialized into the ethos of the group. There is one facet of this tradition, however, that was not shared by every ancient culture. It can be found expressed in the writings of the prophets. There we find the notion of God's universal embrace of all peoples, all nations, and all cultures: "In days to come . . . all nations shall stream toward [the house of the LORD]" (Isa 2:2; Mic 4:1). The manner in which this will be accomplished is clearly stated in the New Testament: "Go, therefore, and make disciples of all nations" (Matt 28:19).

An introduction not only will explain *how* the Bible was written but also will reveal *how* and *why* the people handed down its traditions: "All scripture is inspired by God and is useful for teaching, for refutation, for correction, and for training in righteousness" (2 Tim 3:16). There are some questions that an introduction cannot answer, because historical or literary tools cannot probe them. They are questions of the validity of the religious claims found in the Bible. Is the perception of God found within the Bible true and valid for our time? Are the values that the Bible promotes relevant to our day? Are the aspirations worthy of our commitment? In other words, is the Bible the word of God for us? These are questions of faith. All an introduction can do is lay out the riches of the tradition. It is up to the reader to step across the threshold into the acceptance of faith.

Part I

In Human Words

Before we discuss what it means to say that the word of God comes to us in human words, we must be clear about the historical character of biblical religion. In the years before Vatican II, most people came to know about the Bible through a collection of biblical stories then called *Bible History*. These stories were often read quite literally and understood as accounts of actual historical events. With the coming of Vatican II, we were directed to employ historical-critical approaches in reading the biblical texts in order to uncover the meaning intended by the original authors. As a consequence of this new approach to understanding the Bible, what was once thought to be human history was now considered "salvation history." In other words, the Bible contains not merely the history of human events, but the history of God's action in and through those events.

This understanding of the Bible maintains that human history, with all of its joys and sorrows, its successes and failures, its discoveries and losses, is not the primary focus of the biblical stories. Rather, human history is a lens through which we look as we try to discover how our religious ancestors understood their relationship with God as it unfolded within their particular history. This religious approach in no way minimizes the significance of human history. On the contrary, it underscores its importance. It insists that what came to be known as biblical religion was shaped by a combination of the geographic, social, and political circumstances within which the people lived, the ways in which various aspects of their culture shaped their understanding and behavior, and their interaction with other nations. Because biblical religion bears the mark of history, then that history must be examined if the meaning of its religion is to be grasped.

In order to understand how the Bible is the word of God in human words, we must examine the way religious traditions developed out of the history of ancient Israel and early Christianity. This task will take us through a long and labyrinthian process. We will try to uncover a process that began with people reflecting on events of life, interpreting their meaning, and transmitting this interpretation generation after generation. This tradition would include any necessary adjustment of elements needed to make it relevant to new generations. This tradition would be combined with other meaningful traditions as various groups consolidated to make one people; and it would include the reinterpretation of those traditions threatened by some crisis of understanding and, finally, the recognition of the traditions' revelatory significance. This entire process was accomplished through both oral and written transmission.

Chapter 1

Out of History

The history that undergirds our biblical tradition can be divided into several quite discrete historical periods: the time of the tribes; the time of the monarchy, first united and then divided; postexilic Israel; the Hellenistic period; and the Roman period. The biblical traditions developed out of the events that occurred during these periods, and they reflect many historical features.

The Tribes of Israel

The history of Israel is frequently traced back to the time when Abram was called by God to leave his home in Mesopotamia and travel west to a land that God would show him. There Abram and his descendants would become a great nation (Gen 12:1-2). That nation was, of course, Israel, and Abram, whose name was changed to Abraham, was revered as one of the nation's primary ancestors. Despite the importance of this tradition, most scholars maintain that the history of Israel began when various tribes and groups of people organized themselves into a functioning federation in an identifiable tract of land. This took place during a time known as the period of the judges (1220–1050 BCE), and it occurred in the land of Canaan. The people in question included groups known as "the Kenites, the Kenizzites, the Kadmonites, the Hittites, the Perizzites, the Rephaim, [and] the Amorites" (Gen 15:19-21), as well as the "Hittites, Hivites, Perizzites, Girgashites, Amorites and Jebusites" (Josh 3:10). There were clans such as Ephraim, Benjamin, Machir, Zebulun, Reuben, Dan, Asher, and Naphtali, to name but a few (Judg 5:14-18).

3

As is the case with all people, these groups and clans cherished stories about the ancestors to whom they owed their origin. Some of the stories explain the movement of ancestors from place to place. We see this in the accounts of the nomadic lives of the households of Abraham and Sarah, Isaac and Rebekah, Jacob and Leah and Rachel (Gen 12–50). Other stories tell how God promised first Abram and then Isaac and Jacob that they would eventually have a land of their own (Gen 12:1-3; 26:3; 35:12). There are stories that recount how the ancestors visited or even established important shrines at Shechem (Gen 12:6-7), Bethel (12:8), Mamre (13:18), and Beer-sheba (21:33). Such stories not only established the religious reputation of the ancestors but also laid claim on the religious sites themselves. If the ancestors set up altars to God in these places, surely their descendants could claim some form of property rights. Another story that establishes property rights is the account of Abraham's purchase of a burial place for his wife Sarah (23:17-20).

We are not sure how these ancestral stories actually originated. Since many of them are associated with such places as shrines, scholars believe that the stories may have been remembered, handed down, and reinterpreted there. It was at these shrines that various groups entered into alliances with each other. These alliances, called covenants, were religious pacts by means of which the members promised to be faithful to God and to support each other in times of need. When necessary, groups would meet in religious assembly to renew their commitment to God and to each other. An example of this is found in the account of the entry into the land of Canaan (Josh 24:25-27).

Since people changed location and shifted social and political allegiance quite frequently at this time in history, ancestral stories of one group often overlapped with those of another. As the people themselves amalgamated, their traditions were brought together into a common story. In that common story, Abraham, "the father of a host of nations" (Gen 17:5), became the first ancestor. Jacob, whose name was changed to Israel (32:29), became the immediate predecessor of the twelve tribes who formed the basis of the nation of Israel. The stories of Isaac seem simply to link these two major traditions.

A collection of quite dramatic stories, which probably belonged to only one group of people who entered the land, has come to be known as the Moses tradition. It tells of a group of people who migrated to Egypt during an unusually severe famine. Though conditions eventually improved, some of their number remained in that land and grew to be quite powerful; but with the death of a pharaoh who had been accepting of them and the accession to the throne of one who was not, their lot changed from prosperity to marginalization. Egyptian history substantiates many of the details of this story; but the Israelite account interprets them in a very different way. According to the Egyptian version, Pharaoh Akhenaton closed all of the temples dedicated to the traditional Egyptian gods, and he enforced the worship of one deity. At his death, his religion was crushed, the ancient shrines were reopened, and the land was purged of foreign influences.

The Israelites tell how the one true God responded to the cries of the oppressed people, challenged the divine power of the pharaoh in his own territory, and, under the leadership of Moses, led the people out of Egyptian servitude, across a desert expanse, and into a land that they would claim as their own. These two accounts are probably not the same story, but the similarities between the two cannot be denied. The Egyptian history may have served as the backdrop of the Israelite story of deliverance.

According to the Moses tradition, God made a covenant with this people, promising to protect them and requiring obedience from them. Since Egyptian power and influence extended beyond its borders and encompassed the land of Canaan in its domain, people living there under Egyptian control would have been enthralled by a story that emphasized Egyptian vulnerability. Archaeologists have discovered the remains of a library containing correspondence between Egyptian officials and Canaanite rulers who report unrest in the land at this time. This suggests that the Moses people were entering the land of Canaan at about the same time that the people there were ready to rebel against Egyptian overlordship. The story of deliverance from Egypt would have captured the essence of the experience of those in the land, even though the details of the account differed from their memory.

This Moses tradition was eventually incorporated into the now common ancestral account. To the stories about Abraham, Isaac, and Jacob was added yet another set of stories. This latter tradition featured Jacob's son Joseph, who was sold into slavery in Egypt by his brothers. Some of these stories resemble the Egyptian tradition about an outsider who rose to power and whose death signaled the expulsion of foreign influence. The tribes that were eventually identified as the descendants of the twelve sons of Jacob soon had a common story. It began with the arrival in Canaan of their ancestors from Haran, recorded their movements throughout Canaan, explained their time in Egypt, and chronicled their journey from that land back to Canaan. Most likely, no one group experienced all of these events. Yet, some group or groups probably experienced each of the events. As they fashioned themselves into a united federation, their individual stories merged into one. This was probably the first step in the development of what eventually came down to us as the Bible.

As the diverse groups were forming themselves into a federation of tribes and their various traditions were becoming a common narrative, stories about events actually taking place at that time were being formed as well. These events had to do with the exercise of social and political power, the shifting of tribal allegiances, and the occupation of the land of Canaan. Most of these stories are reports of military engagements in which the people of God forcibly took control of territory in the land of Canaan (Josh 1–12). A few stories indicate that alliances were made with the people of the land (9:15), thus precluding armed conflict. Finally, some accounts, such as the report of the crossing of the Jordan River at Gilgal (5:1-12), suggest a relatively uneventful infiltration of the land. It may well be that the people chose to preserve more accounts of armed conflict than of simple settlement because these, more than other traditions, dramatically demonstrated God's action on behalf of the people.

The Monarchy

The tribal agreement known as covenant proved too weak to hold them to their promise of mutual protection. When the call for help rang out over the land, not everyone responded: "Curse Meroz . . . For they came not to my help" (Judg 5:23). When Saul heard that another city was languishing without assistance from its covenant partners, he threatened to punish those Israelites who did not rally to his battle call (1 Sam 11:17). Incidents like these showed the urgent need for some form of centralized leadership. In the ancient world, this meant monarchy. Such a form of government may have appeared to be the only political choice if the people were to survive attacks from more powerful neighbors. For religious reasons, however, a monarchy was unacceptable.

At this time in the ancient Near East, the king was thought to be either the direct descendant of a god or a god in human form. The Israelites had one God and were not willing to bestow any divine prerogatives on a mere human ruler. Thus they were faced with a dilemma: survival as a people, or faithfulness to the God with whom they were bound by covenant. Though it probably took more than one generation, the people retained their covenant relationship with their God and successfully developed an acceptable understanding of royal ideology. They established a form of monarchy in which the king was still seen as intimately related to God yet was bound by the covenant law like every other Israelite: "I will be a father to him, and he shall be a son to me. And if he does wrong, I will correct him with the rod of men and with human chastisements" (2 Sam 7:14).

Saul, the first king, was more like a wide-reaching military leader than a royal administrator. He ruled the northern tribes of Israel. David, the second king, established himself as both military leader and royal administrator. He was first crowned king of Judah by the southern tribes (2 Sam 2:4). Under David, groups of diverse backgrounds and loyalties were united. After Saul's death, the northern tribes became disappointed with the administration of Saul's son Ishbaal and called David to be king of Israel as well (5:3). When David captured the Jebusite city of Jerusalem, he made it the capital of his dual kingdom (5:6-7). Relative peace reigned in the ancient Near Eastern world at this time, and so David was able to consolidate his power, constitute an administrative government, and expand the territory over which he had control. He guaranteed that royal rule would remain in his family line by establishing a dynasty, and he received divine approbation of it: "Your house and your kingdom shall endure forever before me; your throne shall stand firm forever" (7:16).

The Davidic monarchy is credited with not only political successes but religious accomplishments as well. Chief among them is probably the transfer of the ark of the covenant to Jerusalem, thus according that city the religious importance earlier enjoyed by the tribal shrines. To further reinforce the religious legitimacy of the monarchy, many of the ancestral stories were reinterpreted from a Davidic point of view. (Since the nineteenth century, this theological perspective has been known as the Yahwist or J [Jahwist in German] tradition.) An example of this reinterpretation is the story of Abram's encounter with Melchizedek, the king of Salem (a shortened form of Jerusalem). This mysterious figure was also a priest of God Most High, the name of the god worshiped by the people of that city before David's conquest of it. Abram paid homage to the king of Salem (Gen 14:18-20). The story might suggest that, if our renowned ancestor can revere the king of Jerusalem, we certainly can too.

David's son Solomon succeeded him as king of both Judah and Israel. Solomon embarked on several building projects, chief among which was the temple in Jerusalem. As splendorous as these projects might have been, their financial outlay gave rise to heavy taxation. The northern part of the kingdom was particularly burdened. When Solomon died and his successor sought to secure the allegiance of the elders of the northern tribes, they demanded that he reduce their financial burden. When he refused, they disaffiliated themselves from the monarchy: "What share have we in David? We have no heritage in the son of Jesse. To your tents, O Israel! Now look to your own house, David" (1 Kgs 12:16). The kingdom that had been united under David was now split (922 BCE). A member of the David family ruled in Judah, and Jeroboam was named king in Israel.

The secession of Israel from Davidic rule was viewed by the southern kingdom as apostasy, and the northern kings were condemned as sinners: "He did evil in the sight of the LORD, not desisting from the sins which Jeroboam, son of Nabat, had caused Israel to commit" (2 Kgs 15:9; see also 3:2; 9:9; 10:29; 13:2; 14:16; 15:18, 24, 28; 17:22). On the other hand, the northern kingdom judged the Davidic monarchy's exploitation as disloyalty to the fundamental covenant associated with Moses. As their battle cry indicated, they claimed fidelity to the Mosaic tradition, and they reinterpreted the ancestral stories from that point of view. (This second version of the ancestral stories came to be known as the Elohist or E tradition.)

These two kingdoms ruled independently of each other for about two hundred years. At times they were allied and there was even intermarriage; at other times they aligned themselves on opposite sides of international conflict. Their separation was political, not religious. Both kingdoms continued to worship the same God, though at different shrines. They both considered themselves covenant partners with God, and they observed the same religious laws. They revered the same ancestors, and basically they cherished the same religious history.

As these events unfolded in Israel and Judah, both Egypt and Assyria were gaining power and extending that power across the Fertile Crescent, with these two minor kingdoms in their paths. Assyria became more aggressive and invaded the kingdom of Israel (722 BCE) Hezekiah, king of Judah, negotiated with the Assyrian king and Judah was spared. The southern kingdom interpreted the northern defeat as punishment from God for seceding from Davidic rule, and they saw their own delivery from harm as evidence of God's protection of them because they were blameless. Since the split of the kingdoms had been basically political and the political power of the North was now destroyed, the religious loyalties of northern worshipers were reunited to those of the South. Worship of the God of Israel was once again centralized in Jerusalem. Northern theology, however, was not lost. Many of the Elohist stories were incorporated into the Yahwist tradition, thus producing what has come to be referred to as JE. This explains why sometimes the Bible contains two versions of the same story. An example of this is the story of Abraham concealing the identity of his wife Sarah so that his life would be spared by the Egyptians (Gen 12:10-20 [J]; 20:1-18 [E]).

Though he was forced to capitulate to Assyria, Hezekiah did attempt a reform in Judah: "It was he who removed the high places, shattered the pillars, and cut down the sacred poles [all pagan shrines]" (2 Kgs 18:4). The book of Proverbs contains evidence of literary activity at this time: "These also are proverbs of Solomon. The men of Hezekiah, king of Judah, transmitted them" (Prov 25:1). A later Judean king, Josiah, initiated a second reform. During this time a copy of the book of the covenant was found in the temple. This may have been a draft of covenant law that originated in the North and was brought down to the South after defeat by the Assyrians and later formed the core of the tradition known as Deuteronomic (D). Josiah based his reform on the contents of this book.

The history of the nation from the period of the judges down to the time of Josiah was now viewed through the lens of the Law. The nation's success was seen as reward for compliance with the Law; its failure as punishment for defiance. An obvious example of this is found in the stories of the judges. Disobedience resulted in defeat by some enemy; repentance was blessed with a savior who would rescue the people (Judg 3:7-9). The same was true with stories about the monarchy as seen in the judgment against the northern kings. The evaluation of Josiah reflects fundamental Deuteronomic theology: "Before him there had been no king who turned to the LORD as he did, with his whole heart, his whole soul, and his whole strength, in accord with the entire law of Moses; nor could any after him compare with him" (2 Kgs 23:25). This appraisal is almost identical to a passage found in the book of Deuteronomy: "[Y]ou shall love the LORD, your God, with all your heart, and with all your soul, and with all your strength" (Deut 6:5).

The reform of Josiah notwithstanding, Judah fell to the more powerful forces of Babylon that marched down the western corridor of the Fertile Crescent just as Assyria had done earlier. In the course of three waves of invasion (597, 587, and 582 BCE), the kingdom of Judah was defeated and a large segment of the population was taken into exile in Babylon. The glories of the kingdom established by David and embellished by Solomon were crushed; the religious understanding of monarchy that developed throughout the monarchic period seemed devoid of meaning;

the people were confused and disheartened. The exile would prove to be the crucible in which the people would either lose their identity or refashion it in a new way.

During the entire period of the monarchy one group of people acted as the conscience of the nation. They were the prophets. From the time of the prophet Samuel, who anointed first Saul (1 Sam 10:1) and then David (16:13) as king, to the time of Ezekiel, who ministered during the time of the exile (Ezek 1:1), individuals called the people to covenant fidelity. Only stories about prophets like Deborah (Judg 4:4), Samuel (1 Sam 3:20), Nathan (2 Sam 7:2), and Huldah (2 Kgs 22:14) were handed down. Other prophets are better known because their disciples preserved their prophetic messages, which are found in books that bear their names. Amos and Hosea prophesied to the people in the northern kingdom; Isaiah, Micah, and Jeremiah prophesied to those in the South.

Postexilic Israel

The exile was not only a political disaster causing great social upheaval; it also called into question much of the major theology of the people. If, as the royal theology claimed, God had chosen the family of David to rule "firm forever" (2 Sam 7:13), how was one to explain the collapse of the monarchy and the defeat of the nation? Was God not strong enough to protect the people? Had God gone back on the promises made? Or, had the promises been spurious all the time? And what could be said about the presence of God in the midst of the people? From the time of the judges, the people had been confident that God was in their midst. The ark of the covenant symbolized this presence first in the wilderness, then within the portable tabernacle that David set up, and finally within the temple built by Solomon. Not only had the temple been destroyed but, according to one of Ezekiel's visions, the glory of God left the temple before its destruction (Ezek 8:6). Had God forsaken the people?

The defeat by the Babylonians suggested to many Israelites that the Babylonian gods had defeated the God of Israel, and so they transferred their allegiance to those gods. One group of loyal Israelites, referred to as "the remnant," clung fast to their covenant commitment and began the long and challenging task of looking anew at both the tenets of faith and the religious practices that flowed from them. The Deuteronomistic History that had taken shape before the exile was now edited again. Its basic theme of retribution (fidelity is rewarded; infidelity is punished) provided a theological explanation of their plight. The exile had shattered the reliance the people had placed in the monarchy. Now they realized that their only sure protection could be found in God. Thus, fidelity to the Law replaced dependence on the king.

With no temple in which to offer sacrifice, the people in exile gave more prominence to religious practices that did not require a place of worship. This included strict observance of dietary laws and social customs, attention to prayer, and communal study of the Law. The gathering of the people for prayer and study developed into what came to be known as the synagogue. The final editing of the preexilic traditions was probably accomplished at this time. The ancestral narratives that comprised the JE ancestral tradition were appended to the exilic version of the Deuteronomistic History (D). This national story was then prefaced by a collection of etiological tales that provided explanations of the origins of certain customs (Gen 4:21-22), extraordinary life circumstances (11:1-9), and of humankind itself (1:26-28; 2:7, 21-22). Scholars believe that the final editors placed these traditions within a literary framework that emphasized cultic practices such as observance of the Sabbath (2:2-3). This editorial tradition is called Priestly (P). The combination of all these traditions is often referred to as JEDP. Israel now had a story that opened with creation itself (Gen 1:1), recounted its journey from tribal organization to monarchy, and ended with a Judean king in exile (2 Kgs 25:30).

Besides the final compilation and editing of the national story, the writings of the preexilic prophets were also edited, if only slightly, so that their messages would be relevant to those who had experienced the terrors of the exile and were free to rebuild their lives. This editing explains passages filled with hope in an otherwise challenging book like Jeremiah: "The days are coming, says the LORD, when I will make a new covenant with the house of Israel and the house of Judah" (Jer 31:31). The task of rebuilding the nation and reestablishing religious customs and practices of worship was daunting. The books of Ezra and Nehemiah recount the people's initial excitement and their eventual disillusionment. Once again, prophetic voices like Obadiah and Zechariah urged them on.

The people who returned from the exile realized that they would have to live in their land in ways different than did the generation that was taken into exile in the first place. Since, from their religious point of view, the exile was actually punishment for their breach of covenant commitment, they would have to avoid whatever might threaten that commitment again. If their infidelity had resulted from their appropriation of foreign ideas and customs, then they would be vigilant in rejecting such foreign influence. Some went so far as to require the divorce of foreign wives and the dismissal of children born of them (Ezra 10:3). Others insisted that foreign influences need not turn one away from God. These people went so far as to say that foreigners too could be faithful to God. Stories like Ruth, the Moabite ancestor of David (Ruth 4:17), and the repentance of the hated Ninevites described in the story of Jonah, illustrate their point of view.

During this time of restoration, Israel was really a colony of the Persian Empire. Those who ruled in the land may have been Jews, but they were appointed by the Persian ruler and were accountable to him. A Persian colony had already been established in the land of Israel in the North, with Samaria as its capital. Incorporation of the returnees into this province was inevitable. Many of the people in Samaria were the descendants of Israelites who had intermarried with the Assyrians at the time of the destruction of the northern kingdom (722 BCE). They offered to assist the returnees in the rebuilding of the temple (Ezra 4:1-3). After all, they too were worshipers of the God of Israel. However, since the returnees considered such intermarriage inappropriate, they would have nothing to do with the Samaritans. This so angered the Samaritans that they tried to thwart the reconstruction, which only served to deepen the enmity between the returnees and the Samaritans.

Hellenistic Period

The exploits of the Greek ruler Alexander the Great (356–323 BCE) made an impact on the religious identity of many Jewish people. The conquests of his armies, as consequential as they might have been, paled when compared with the spread of Greek culture (Hellenization) that he was able to effect. At his death, Alexander's empire was divided among his generals: Egypt went to Ptolemy, and Syria went to Seleucus. Since the land of the Jews, now called Palestine, lay between these two kingdoms, the Ptolemies and the Seleucids vied for control of it. The plight of the Jews under the Seleucids is reflected in the books of Maccabees. There we read of the extent of the Hellenization forced on the Jews by Antiochus IV. Under him, the people were forbidden to observe the Sabbath, to follow dietary regulations, and to circumcise their sons. Furthermore, they were required to offer sacrifice to pagan gods. The ultimate sacrilege occurred when an image of the Greek god Zeus was set up in the temple itself.

Jews who insisted on being faithful to their religious practices faced the possibility of death. A touching story of a mother who watched the martyrdom of her seven sons before she herself was put to death recounts the heinousness of the persecution (2 Macc 7). Another story that encourages resistance, even in the face of death, is found on the book of Daniel. Though some later writers, such as the Jewish historian Josephus (Ant. *x.* 11.4, 6) and the author of the Gospel of Matthew (Matt 24:15), classified Daniel with the prophets, he was not really a prophet. Nor is the book that bears his name a book of prophecy. The first part (chaps. 1–6) is a specific kind of Jewish writing called *haggadah*, which is a form of story meant to make a moral point rather than report historical facts. The book of Daniel demonstrates the importance of fidelity to Jewish practices, even in the face of death. The second part of the book (chaps. 7–12) is a unique form of literature known as apocalypse (see "Literary Forms" in chap. 5).

The story of Daniel is set in Babylon during the period of the Israelite exile, but it was written during the time of Antiochus IV. The heroes of the story are loyal Jews who preferred to die rather than repudiate their religious customs. The fidelity and courage of these young men are set before the Jews suffering at the hand of Antiochus IV as examples to follow. The rescue of Daniel and his companions is meant to assure the others that God will rescue them as well. The part of the book of Daniel that might lead some to consider him a prophet describes his visions. Like Joseph who interpreted dreams while he was a captive in Egypt (Gen 40–41), Daniel was able to interpret dreams (Dan 7–12). In both instances, this ability demonstrated the God-given superior wisdom of the imprisoned man of God. In Daniel's case, this wisdom reinforced the case for fidelity.

Extreme and forced Hellenization precipitated outright rebellion, which was led by a family known as Maccabees (1 Macc 2–4). Though outnumbered by the Greeks and lacking comparable military armaments, the Jews launched a kind of guerilla warfare that soon escalated to full-scale military engagement. The fighting lasted for three years, after which most of the city of Jerusalem was recaptured. The altar, once defiled by Antiochus, was rebuilt and rededicated. An eight-day festival marked this rededication (1 Macc 4:36-61). (This festival continues to be commemorated yearly in the eight-day celebration of the feast of Dedication, otherwise known as Hanukkah.) With the defeat of the Greek overlords, the Maccabean family assumed both the political leadership of the people and the office of high priest. This latter act was considered illegitimate by many of the pious Jews and eventually caused some to break away. The Essenes, associated with Qumran during the time of Jesus, are considered descendants of this resistance group.

This period of Jewish history saw the birth of several political and religious sects that we have come to know in the New Testament. The antagonism between Samaritans and Jews has already been discussed. It was at this time that the Hasidim or "pious ones" challenged the right of a political leader to assume the office of high priest. The Essenes were one branch of this Hasidic sect. A second religious sect known as the Pharisees, whose name means "separated ones," were lay interpreters of the Law who also objected to the usurpation of the office of high priest. They resisted the adoption of practices that were not Jewish, and they criticized severely those Jews who were not as observant as they were. A third sect, the Sadducees, came from the wealthy Palestinian aristocracy. While the Pharisees disputed the king's right to usurp the office of high priest, the Sadducees did not seem to protest it. Their wealth and acceptance of the policies of those in power gained them significant social and political prominence in the Jewish community.

A second group of Jews had an entirely different experience of Hellenization. They lived in Egypt under Ptolemaic rule. Though they also struggled with how the culture of their Greek overlords influenced their religious tradition, they did not suffer the kind of persecution that befell their Palestinian cohorts. They appear to have adapted to the culture and prospered. There came a time, however, when they realized that the Hebrew traditions were foreign to them, because they gradually became unfamiliar with the Hebrew language itself. The need to translate these traditions into Greek became quite clear. Yet they considered their religious traditions inspired by God, and they feared that a translation might in some way undermine the sacredness of these writings. A tradition grew up regarding the translation of the sacred texts from Hebrew to Greek. It claimed that seventy scribes set out on the task independent of each other. When the work was finished and the translations compared, they were all found to be identical. Since such a feat was obviously impossible, they concluded that the common translation was clearly inspired. This version came to be known as the Septuagint (LXX), from the Greek word for "seventy."

A preface to the book of Ecclesiasticus or Sirach reports that by this time, the sacred books of the Jews had been organized into three distinct parts called "the law, the prophets, and the rest of the books." The Law consisted of the first five books, today called the Torah by Jews and the Pentateuch by Christians; the prophets included the preexilic historical books containing stories about prophets as well as books with prophetic teachings; the other writings included psalms and wisdom writings and include, among others, the books of Job and Proverbs. This means that by the second century before the Christian era, the sacred writings of the Jewish people had basically achieved the shape that they have today.

As was the case throughout Israel's history, traditions were always being formed, handed down, and reshaped as needed. During the Hellenistic period, many of these traditions were written in Greek. Some of them, such as the Wisdom of Solomon, were eventually added to the collection of inspired writings and became part of the Catholic Bible.

Roman Period

In 63 BCE, Pompey, the Roman general who took control of Damascus, moved in on Jerusalem and captured it. The land was annexed to Rome as part of the province of Syria. Though Roman rule changed hands frequently during these years, the control of Palestine was securely in the hands of the Herodian family. One of the most significant members of this family was a king known from the stories of Jesus' birth—Herod the Great. He ruled for over thirty years, and during that time he launched and completed many spectacular building projects. In order to demonstrate his Roman loyalties, he built temples that honored the emperor, theaters, gymnasia, hippodromes, bathhouses, and even Roman cities like Caesarea. In order to appease the Jewish populations, Herod restored the temple and constructed sturdy walls and a citadel to protect it. The citadel was named Antonia in an effort to please Mark Antony, who had been influential in Herod's rise to power.

Though he exercised considerable power, Herod's position was never totally secure, for it was dependent on his constant alignment and realignment with various Roman dignitaries. This very practice intensified his vulnerability, since Roman political status was always shifting. For his own safety, he built personal fortresses at Machaerus on the northeastern shore of the Dead Sea, at Masada at the western end of the Judean desert also overlooking the Dead Sea, and the Herodium, where he was ultimately buried. It was during the reign of Herod that Jesus was born, despite the fact that this king died in the year 4 BCE. (The discrepancy in the dating of Jesus' birth can be traced back to 525 CE when the reigning pope decided to establish a feast commemorating this event.)

The political intrigue within which the Herodian family was entangled determined the events in the life of Jesus and the development of the traditions that were generated by those events. According to Matthew's gospel, the family of Jesus fled to Egypt because Herod threatened the life of the child (Matt 2:13), and it was word of Herod's death that brought them back to settle in Nazareth (vv. 19-23). Herod's heirs were no less brutal than he was. His son Herod Antipas beheaded John the Baptist in order to fulfill a frivolous promise made during a banquet (Matt 14:3-10; Mark 6:19-28). It was to this same king that Pilate sent the captured Jesus, hoping that Herod would resolve the dilemma that Jesus seemed to have created. Herod allowed his soldiers to scourge and humiliate Jesus (Luke 23:11), but he did not sentence him to death.

The persecution of the followers of Jesus by Herod Agrippa, the grandson of Herod the Great, is found in the Acts of the Apostles. He ordered the death of James, the brother of John, and he then arrested Peter (Acts 12:2-3). After a reign of almost forty-three years, the Roman emperor banished Herod, and Palestine fell under the control of Roman procurators. It was such a procurator named Felix who played an important role in the ministry of Paul. Although the early church inherited traditions that had a decidedly postexilic character, their Roman influence cannot be denied.

Summary

As is the case with all history, the events recorded in the Bible are largely subjective interpretations of what happened in the lives of the people, rather than merely objective reports. They describe how the ancient Israelites and the early Christians understood God's involvement in the events recorded there. Though this religious interpretation is the primary source of our understanding of the actual history that lies behind the biblical story, this does not mean that the history that we have been able to reconstruct is unreliable. The records of other ancient civilizations bear out the authenticity of many biblical accounts. Both the ancient Israelites and the early Christians were more interested in the religious meaning of the events than in their social, political, or economic details. However, we would not be able to appreciate this religious meaning if we did not have an adequate grasp of those social, political, and economic details.

Chapter 2

In a Place

Just as history plays an important role in shaping our understanding of ourselves and our relationships with each other and with God, so geography determines the contours not only of our outer world but of our inner world as well. Geography offers some of the raw material for making meaning. The physical characteristics of the world in which we live are given meaning according to the way we perceive their relevance to our lives. Anthropologists insist that any human group together with its environment constitutes a single interacting ecosystem. In line with this, their chosen religion is influenced by their worldview and it gives meaning to the physical features and relationships of this ecosystem. For example, mountain people view themselves and God in ways quite different than do fisherfolk.

It is not uncommon for people to maintain that some physical feature of their territory is the actual center of the world, or the *axis mundi*. They believe that this axis joins the sky, the earth, and the underworld, and thus enables the gods to descend to earth, and the dead to descend to the subterranean regions. The axis might be a mountain, a tree, a pillar, a significant stone, or some other remarkable natural phenomenon. Nomadic people might determine the axis by planting a pole in the midst of the encampment. As the people move, the axis moves with them. This practice demonstrates the importance of the human community's mapping their universe and giving it meaning. Giving religious meaning to certain geographic features is one way of designating those features as sacred.

Sacred space within the human world is that unique place where the divine and the human worlds explicitly converge and interact. It is a place of divine presence and power, a place of divine revelation. Hence sanctuaries are built there and people pilgrimage to them. Although scared space is located within ordinary space, there is a dimension of it that is otherworldly. When one is in scared space, ordinary pursuits of life are set aside, and one enters the world of the divine. Scared space is usually bounded in some way, so that people know that they are entering another world. Sacred thresholds are observed, people sanctify themselves, and rituals of passage are performed.

A perfect example of sacred space and axis mundi is found in the account of the garden in Eden (Gen 2:8–3:24). Though not explicitly mentioned in the story, there must have been some kind of boundary that distinguished the garden from the rest of Eden. This is clear at the end of the narrative: a guard is placed at the threshold of the garden, preventing the couple from reentering it. The tree of life, placed in the middle of the garden, probably represents the axis mundi (2:9). The sacredness of the garden is marked in two ways. First, it is the place where God and the human beings communicate. Second, it cannot tolerate evil, and so the serpent is punished and the human couple is expelled. This story does not recount actual historical events. Rather, it explains why human beings do not live in a paradise land, and why they always mark off places that are considered sacred where they can meet God.

In traditional societies, as was ancient Israel, habitation itself usually underwent a process of sanctification. The city was considered an *imago mundi* or "image of the world." Since the world itself was a divine creation, so was its imago. This explains the cosmic symbolism found in the very structure of many major ancient cities. This is particularly true with regard to the construction of temples. Temples, more than any other human structure, constituted the imago mundi.

Shrines

The first biblical mention of a shrine is found at the very beginning of the ancestral tradition: "Abram passed through the land as far as the sacred place at Shechem, by the terebinth of Morah" (Gen 12:6). Already a Canaanite shrine, Abram built an altar at Shechem to commemorate the fact that God appeared to him there (v. 7). The terebinth was obviously a sacred tree. (Mamre, another site where Abram built an altar, was also revered because of the sacred tree that grew there [Gen 13:18]).

Shechem is also mentioned in the Jacob tradition (Gen 33:19-20). It was at Shechem that Joshua gathered the people to make a covenant with God upon their entrance into the land (Josh 24:25), and there the bones of Joseph were buried (24:32). It was to Shechem that Solomon's son went, expecting to be proclaimed king. Instead, because he refused to lighten the burden of taxation borne by the people of the North, he was denounced and the northern tribes separated from Davidic rule (1 Kgs 12:1-20). The sacredness of the site conferred a sacred character on the events that took place there. After the exile, when Jerusalem was being rebuilt, Shechem became the religious capital of the Samaritan nation.

Bethel was a second important ancestral shrine. As was the case with Shechem, traditions about both Abram and Jacob are associated with this shrine. It was there that Abram built an altar (Gen 12:8), and it was there that Jacob had a dream of angels moving up and down a staircase to heaven. He is the one who changed its name from Luz to Bethel, which means "house of God" (28:10-19). It continued to be an important shrine site during the time of the judges, particularly because the ark of the covenant, the symbol of God's presence in the midst of the people, was at one time located there (Judg 20:26-27). Once Jerusalem was made the site of the central shrine of the land, Bethel's importance faded. However, with the secession of the northern tribes from Davidic rule, Bethel was reconstituted a major shrine by the northern king. It was to this shrine that the prophet Amos went to deliver the word of the Lord to the people of the North (Amos 7:10-13).

During the time of the judges, sites were revered because they housed the ark of the covenant. This was the case with Gilgal. It was there that the people first set foot in the land of promise, and there that the men were circumcised (Josh 5:2-3). There the people celebrated the first Passover in the land (v. 10), and they ceased to be nourished with manna (v. 12). The name Gilgal means "circle" and probably refers to a circle of stones that marked the shrine that was built there (Josh 4:19-22). The importance of the shrine continued into the time of the monarchy. It was there that Saul was made the first king of Israel (1 Sam 11:15), and it was there that he lost favor with God because he himself offered sacrifice rather than wait for the prophet (1 Sam 13:8-14). Like the other northern shrines, Gilgal was censured by the South for celebrating rites other than at the temple in Jerusalem.

Shiloh replaced Gilgal as a major shrine. The Tent of Meeting was set up there and, presumably, the ark of the covenant was housed in that Tent (1 Sam 1:3, 7). Carrying the ark into major battles was a way of saying that God was with the people, and this presence was considered a guarantee of success. During one momentous battle, the ark was taken from Shiloh and brought to Aphek, which was the place where the Israelite army was encamped (1 Sam 4:4). The battle was a disaster, and the ark was captured. In this way Shiloh ceased to be a major shrine. Much later in history, the prophet Jeremiah used the destruction of Shiloh as a portent of the destruction of the temple in Jerusalem (Jer 7:12-14).

By far, of course, the most significant shrine was the temple in Jerusalem. Built on Mount Zion, it soon appropriated all of the religious symbolism associated with the cosmic mountain. The temple itself faced east, the direction from which illumination came. Because it housed the ark of the covenant, the temple was considered the place where God dwelt in the midst of the people. The presence of the ark in the temple also incorporated the tribal religion of earlier times with the royal theology associated with the monarchy. Jerusalem, and no other site, had come to be revered as the axis mundi, and the temple as the imago mundi. This explains why Judean theology condemns Jeroboam's effort to sever the religious loyalties of the people of the seceded northern kingdom from the temple in Jerusalem by reopening the shrines at Dan and Bethel.

Mount Zion continued to be revered as the privileged shrine site, even after the temple was destroyed by the Babylonians (587 BCE). This explains the determination of those who returned from exile to rebuild the temple on the same site (515 BCE). It was this temple that was desecrated by Antiochus IV Epiphanes (167 BCE) and, with the Maccabean victory, rededicated three years later. In about 20 BCE, Herod the Great set out to completely rebuild this temple. This was the same temple that played such an important role in the life of Jesus. A second shrine, built on Mount Gerizim in the land of the Samaritans, rivaled the importance of Jerusalem. In the valley between Mount Gerizim and Mount Ebal lay the city of Shechem, renowned for its association with Jacob (Gen 33:18-20) and known to Christians because it was there that Jesus spoke with the Samaritan woman about worship at shrines (John 4:19-23). The Samaritan temple was built after those who returned from Babylonian exile refused to allow the Samaritans to help them rebuild the temple in Jerusalem (see "postexilic Israel" in chap.1).

The glory of the temple in Jerusalem did not endure, for it was destroyed during the Roman siege of Jerusalem in 70 CE. Only the Western Wall of the Temple Mount remains intact today, and it is cherished as both a religious and a national monument. The Temple Mount itself is the site of the Dome of the Rock. The third holiest Muslim site, after Mecca and Medina, it is believed to be the place where Mohammed ascended to heaven. Some Jews, perhaps only a small minority of them, believe that a new temple must be built on that site before the end time can dawn.

Cities

Most biblical cities were important because of the shrines that were built either within them or in their vicinity. Other cities held political or military significance. Yet even the military cities possessed some degree of religious significance. This is particularly true of Shechem. Originally an ancestral shrine (Gen 12:7; 33:20) and the place of covenant renewal (Josh 8:30), Shechem became the capital of the northern kingdom of Israel (1 Kgs 12:25). Though destroyed by the Assyrians in 722 BCE, Shechem was rebuilt and became the capital of Samaria and later that nation's religious center.

Jericho was a city in the Jordan Valley about six miles north of the Dead Sea. It first appears in the biblical account of the occupation of the land. The story of Jericho's fall is less a historical report than it is a description of the liturgical reenactment of God's victory (Josh 6:20-26). Though not an Israelite shrine, it was highly regarded as a place where the power of God was manifested through an Israelite military victory. This explains the character of the report of its conquest. Regardless of the military engagement that may have transpired, the people's success was credited to God. It was God who fought for them; it was God who captured the city. That is how they interpreted the event, and that is how they handed down the report of it. The Israelites did not later rebuild this city or occupy it in any major way, perhaps because it retained some of its Canaanite practices as a way of securing the safety of the city (1 Kgs 16:34).

Jericho gained prominence again during the time of the Hasmonean kings, the royal family that ruled Israel from 166–37 BCE, after the Maccabean revolt. Herod the Great constructed an elaborate winter palace there. Jesus seems to have visited Jericho on several occasions. It was the site where he healed the blind man (Mark 10:46-52; Luke 18:35-43; [two men in Matt 20:29-34]). It was there that Jesus encountered Zacchaeus (Luke 19:1-10). The danger that lurked in the roads surrounding Jericho is depicted in the story of the Good Samaritan (Luke 10:29-37).

Megiddo, originally a Canaanite city, was captured by the Israelites shortly after they came into the land. It was probably at Megiddo that Deborah and Barak met and defeated the Canaanites (Judg 4:7, 13;

5:19-21). Because of its strategic position, the city became particularly significant for Israel during the time of Solomon. Cities had to be built near a water supply, and Megiddo drew its water from two springs. The settlement itself was constructed on a mound that rose above the neighboring land within which ran the main highway between Egypt and Mesopotamia, known as the Via Maris, or Sea Route. Thus, Megiddo exercised significant control over this highway. In times of danger it became an important military fortress.

Megiddo is also remembered as the site of the defeat of King Josiah (2 Kgs 23:29). The sudden death of this righteous king threw the kingdom of Judah into deep mourning. A much later prophet, Zechariah, compares this national grief with some future mourning that the inhabitants of Jerusalem will have to face (Zech 12:11). This tradition about future distress developed into the eschatological (end-time) tradition of Armageddon, the place where the kings of the earth will muster for the final battle before the coming of the Day of the Lord (Rev 16:16). The word Armageddon probably comes from the Hebrew *har* (mountain) of Megiddon. It seems that the anguish caused by the death of a beloved king, who was a relatively insignificant actor on the ancient Near Eastern world stage, grew to be the symbol of the final anguish that will be faced by the entire human race.

Bethlehem is well known to most people because of the Christmas story. Yet the city enjoyed a history that can be traced as far back as the ancestor Jacob himself. When his beloved wife Rachel died, Jacob buried her near the north entry of the city (Gen 35:19). This burial spot presumes that Jacob possessed some form of property rights (Gen 23:19; 49:31). Thus, since the time of the ancestors, Bethlehem was connected with Israel. The name Bethlehem means "house of bread," reflecting the fertile slopes to the west of the city. The city appears in various tribal stories, but it is the Davidic tradition that solidified the city's importance. Bethlehem was the family home of David (1 Sam 16:1), and the place where he was anointed king (vv. 4-13). The later prophet Micah, when promising a future restoration of the people after great distress, announced the coming from Bethlehem of a new Davidic king (Mic 5:1). Gospel writers see this prophecy fulfilled in the birth of Jesus in Bethlehem (Matt 2:1; Luke 2:4-7).

The most important city in Israel was, of course, Jerusalem. Since the time when David designated this originally Jebusite city as the capital of his newly organized kingdom, Jerusalem was the unrivaled center of Israelite life. Besides being the central shrine of the people, it was also the seat of political power. When the Greek Antiochus IV Epiphanes sought to crush Jewish resistance, he captured Jerusalem; when the Romans overran the territory, they exercised control in Jerusalem. Even when the Jews lost control of the city, it became the symbol of Jewish identity and the hope of Jewish restoration. The early Christians looked to Jerusalem as the cradle of their religion (Acts 1:8) and the symbol of eventual fulfillment (Rev 21:2).

According to the Acts of the Apostles, the Gospel of Jesus spread from Jerusalem to Judea and Samaria, and then to the ends of the earth (Acts 1:8). One city that epitomizes the extraordinary spread of the Good News is Corinth. It was situated on an isthmus between the mainland of Greece and the Peloponnesian Peninsula. It was the most important western port, controlling much of the trade of the nation. At the time of Paul, Corinth was a cosmopolitan city five times the size of Athens. Its location and international character made it the ideal center for Paul's missionary activities. These same characteristics opened the city to various forms of undisciplined living.

Throughout the entire New Testament period, the city that constantly looms on the horizon is Rome. At first it represented the conquerors and the rule of the colonizing power; but in the writings of Paul, himself a Roman citizen (Acts 22:27), Rome represented the threshold to the rest of the world (Acts 19:21). Paul would use the Roman system of travel and communication to spread the Gospel. Though he was not able to realize his dream, other Christians carried the Gospel to the ends of the earth.

Culture

If geography identifies *where* we stand in the world, culture describes *how* we stand there. In fact, culture has often been referred to as "social location." Culture is a system of shared beliefs, values, and behaviors that helps people to make sense of time and space, and that constitutes continuity of group identity from one generation to the next. Chief among the factors that constitute culture are: language, gender, race/ethnicity, and class.

Language

Most people take language for granted. Yet language is a complex set of symbols that express ideas and enable people to think and to communicate with one another. It enables us to describe reality by ascribing symbols or words to it, symbols agreed upon by the group, so that members of the group have a common basis for understanding and communication. Different groups may perceive the same reality but ascribe different words to it. Thus a friendly, small four-legged animal that wags its tail might be called *chien* by the French, *hund* by the Germans, and *dog* by the English.

We really know the world only in terms of the language system of our culture. This is why people are lost in another culture when they do not know what the natives are saying. On the other hand, we also fashion our world according to the language we use to describe it. Respectful and loving language builds people up ("You are number one in my book"), while discriminatory and hateful language tears them down ("You will never amount to anything"). Language indicates who is in and who is outside of the group. It names roles that determine social structures (king, president, principal), and it indicates relationships (mother, father, wife, husband). Concepts borrowed from one language for another expand the scope of the receiving language. Sometimes the foreign word actually becomes part of the second language. The French word *milieu* is an example of this. Without being translated, it has been incorporated into the English language.

The Bible has come down to us in two languages, Hebrew and Greek. The Jews believed that the words of their sacred religious traditions were the words of God, handed down to them through inspired individuals. With the process of Hellenization that took place in the ancient world with the conquests of Alexander the Great, Greek became the spoken language of many Jews living outside of the land of Israel. In this situation, their facility with Hebrew became quite limited. When it became clear that this was leading to the distancing from their religious texts themselves, a group of scholars in Alexandria, Egypt set out to translate these texts into Greek. As noted earlier, tradition grew up claiming that, though separated from each other, seventy translators produced exactly the same version. According to the tradition, this marvel demonstrated that the Greek translation, known now as the Septuagint (LXX), was actually inspired by God and, therefore, an authoritative version for use.

Gender

Gender refers to the way a group identifies and understands the differences between female and male. Though both sexuality and gender are somehow rooted in sexual characteristics, these terms are not identical. Sexuality is determined by nature; gender develops culturally. Each social group defines specific gender roles. For example, since men are the usual warriors, and since warriors need to be aggressive, aggressiveness is often considered a masculine characteristic. In like manner, since women are usually the primary nurturers of young children, nurturing is often considered a feminine characteristic. Patriarchy (father-headed society) was the prominent social structure during the entire biblical period. Thus the gender roles of both ancient Israel and early Christianity demonstrate this patriarchal point of view.

In addition to the patriarchal social structure of ancient Israel and early Christianity, the biblical stories themselves reveal a definite androcentric (male-centered) point of view. The important stories recount the feats of men; the leaders and heroes described are men; even the chief images of God developed by the people are male. The fact that so few women in the biblical stories are named or even mentioned is further evidence that they were undervalued in those androcentric societies. Since the Bible is the word of God in human words, we should not be surprised to find such cultural characteristics in it. The challenge before us consists in looking beyond the cultural limitations in order to discover the religious meaning of the tradition.

Race/Ethnicity

What is today considered racial identity does not seem to have been as important to the people of biblical times as was ethnicity. Though these terms are often used interchangeably, ethnicity is generally understood as group identity that presumes common origin and religion, shared heritage and language. It includes those aspects of a group that are regarded as distinctive and are expressed in language and literature, art and music, family life, public life, and religion.

Several of the characteristics that comprise ethnicity are prominent in the Old Testament. Though various ancestors may actually have been totally distinct from others, in the final version of the story, they are all bound together by ties of common blood. In this way, later generations were able to claim a common story of origin. The insistence of one and the same religion is basic to the ancient Israelites' understanding of themselves as a people chosen by God. In fact, this monotheistic perspective became the lens through which they constantly evaluated their fidelity to the covenant that bound them to God and to each other.

Ethnic commonality plays a significantly different role in the New Testament. In the early chapters of the Christian story, the traditional ethnic separation is apparent. In fact, there seems to have been a question about whether Jesus' ministry should reach out beyond the confines of the Jewish community (Matt 15:21-28). When this question was resolved, a further one arose. Were Gentile converts required to become members of the Jewish community before they could be accepted into the church (Acts 15:1)? Issues such as these demonstrate the struggle between exclusive ethnicity and openness to diversity.

Class

Another notable aspect of culture is class. Class designation and hierarchy are decided by the group. In some groups, class stratification is determined by occupation (the chief, the religious leader, the warrior, etc.). In others, economic status plays the most significant role in deciding class (the wealthy, the poor, and all the people in between). In most cases, there is a convergence of these aspects: those in the most important positions are also the wealthiest. Class status can be either ascribed or achieved. On the one hand, one can be born into the upper class. In many groups, certain families or tribes are automatically considered the leaders. The Windsors in Britain are an example of this. In ancient Israel, both the monarchy (2 Sam 7:13) and the priesthood (Exod 28:1) were inherited positions.

Social class can also be achieved though education, occupation, or skill. A biblical example of this can be seen in the prestige gained by the Maccabees as they successfully held off the forces of Antiochus IV Epiphanes. An example from the New Testament would be the esteem garnered by Jesus though his preaching and healing. It should be clear that achieved status can be easily lost if one loses whatever it was that enabled one to achieve status in the first place.

Closely associated with this sense of status is the notion of "honor and shame." Honor is the claim to worth that is publicly acknowledged by one's group; shame is just the opposite. If one's honor is challenged, one must defend it or be publicly shamed. In patriarchal societies, honor is usually ascribed to or achieved by the adult male only. All other members of the patriarchal household benefit from his honorable status, and they are required to live and act in ways that will not shame or dishonor him. This struggle of honor and shame can be seen in many of Jesus' encounters with the leaders of the people. Whenever they tried to dishonor him before the people, he shamed them.

This short overview of some of the aspects of culture demonstrates the importance of understanding the context out of which developed the theological themes and practices found in the Bible. We must never forget that reading the Bible is actually a cross-cultural exercise. In order to understand what is being communicated to us, we must take into consideration the cultural character of its expression. Authentic and meaningful biblical interpretation requires that we first understand what it originally meant and then reshape that meaning in ways that can be relevant today.

Summary

We cannot easily separate people from the geography of their lives. Their concept of the world is shaped by the characteristics of the particular location in which they live. They experience life in very specific surroundings, and these surroundings carry great significance for them. Often memories are preserved at these sites, and people return to them in order to recall and to celebrate the meaning of those events. This explains the importance that many sites held for the ancient Israelites and the early Christians. They often set up shrines as memorials, and they returned there to worship. Cities were cherished because of the residents' encounters with God that occurred within their boundaries. Geography became sacred. Geography also shapes the interior landscape of communities of human beings, fashioning the cultural characteristics of a people. If we are to appreciate the religious tradition we have inherited from the ancient Israelites and the early Christians, we must understand the world out of which it grew.

Chapter 3

About God

We have already seen that, while the biblical tradition developed out of the historical experiences of the ancient Israelites and the early Christians, the Bible itself is not really a book of history. It is a book of theology. It reveals how people of faith believed that God acted in their lives. Knowing this, we will then appreciate how the religious faith and practices that developed were ways of responding to God's graciousness. In order to understand their beliefs and practices, we must look first at the various ways these believers envisioned God. It is important to remember that all of these characterizations of God are metaphors. They do not really tell us what God is, but what God is like. After we have examined some of the major metaphors or characterizations of God we will better understand the intimate relationship that God initiated with the people in the Bible, a relationship known as covenant. This kind of an examination will provide us with insight into their prayer, which was their response to God's revelation.

Images of God

Deliverer
The earliest and probably the principal way that the ancient Israelites perceived God was as deliverer. Tracing their history as a people back to their escape from Egypt, the Israelites believed that it was God who delivered them from their bondage and made them God's own people: "You have seen for yourselves how I treated the Egyptians and

how I bore you up on eagle wings and brought you here to myself" (Exod 19:4). Deliverance from Egypt was given as the reason for their adherence to the Law (Exod 20:2; Deut 5:6). Acknowledgment of this is found again and again in their religious traditions, particularly in their prayers (Pss 78:43-53; 105:23-38; 135:9; etc.). The development of such a characterization of God is a perfect example of how experience influences theology.

The characterization or image of God as deliverer is augmented by a phrase that captures the forcefulness of God's manner of deliverance: "with [a] strong hand and outstretched arm" (Deut 4:34; 5:15; 7:19; 26:8; Ps 136:12; Jer 32:21; Ezek 20:33-34). This is a military image, one that suggests a battle in which God was victorious. A careful reading of the biblical story shows that it was not merely the Egyptians whom God defeated, but the Pharaoh, the ruler who was thought to be somehow divine. In other words, the struggle between the Israelites and the Egyptians was really a struggle between the God of Israel and the presumed divine powers of Egypt. God was able to deliver the Israelites because God was mightier than those powers.

Warrior

Having delivered the Israelites from Egypt and into the land of promise, God the deliverer is seen in a slightly different form and is more explicitly a warrior, one who fights on the side of the Israelites. Again, it was Israel's experience of conquest and/or defense that reshaped this image of God. Believing that it was God's will that they occupy the land, they were convinced that God was with them, even leading them, as they fought those nations that stood in the way of their accomplishing this feat (Josh 8:1; Judg 4:14). They enacted this belief liturgically by actually bringing the ark of the covenant, the religious object that symbolized God's presence in their midst, into the military camp (1 Sam 4:2-5). The image of God as warrior is prominent in prayers that rejoice in God's victory over the forces of evil: "The LORD is a warrior, / the LORD is his name" (Exod 15:3); "Who is this king of glory? / The LORD, a mighty warrior, / the LORD, mighty in battle" (Ps 24:8).

Another image that captures the same meaning as warrior is *savior*. Although this image is found in the writings of ancient Israel, particularly in Isaiah (Isa 43:3; 45:21; 60:16), the characterization became quite common during the Christian period. There, however, the danger from which God saves is the consequence of sin. This shift in meaning probably results from the influence of Greek thinking. Ancient Hebrew thought favored concrete concepts and imagery, while the Greeks were known for their abstract ponderings.

These images of God as deliverer, warrior, or savior clearly exemplify certain important characteristics of God. First, they underscore God's particular care for the people. When they were in distress, God came to their rescue. In addition to this, the images demonstrate God's sovereignty over all other powers. When God was protecting the people, nothing could overcome them. These theological concepts continue to be cherished by the people of God, even though they might be expressed in different ways using other images.

As stated above, the primary battle that God the "warrior" fought and won was over the cosmic forces of evil. The unfolding of such a drama is found in various early creation myths of the ancient Near Eastern world. The basic story tells of a young, vigorous warrior who stands up to overwhelming cosmic forces that are usually characterized as water monsters. These forces are depicted in this way because of the people's fear of unruly and chaotic waters that may have threatened them when the Tigris and Euphrates rivers overflowed. In the myth, once the battle has been fought and won, the young warrior establishes order in the universe by assigning the celestial beings—the sun, the moon, and the stars, thought to be divine beings themselves—their proper place in the heavens. A palace is then erected for the triumphant warrior-creator god, and it is from this celestial throne that he rules over heaven and earth.

Creator

Although ancient Israel would reject the notion of divine peers that might threaten the sovereignty of its God, it did retain many details of this myth of creation, ascribing them to God as creator and incorporating them in many of their psalms: "When I see your heavens, the work of your fingers, / the moon and stars that you set in place" (Ps 8:4); "the LORD's throne is in heaven" (Pss 11:4; 103:19; etc.). In other poetic passages, references to this cosmic battle are employed to assure the people that in the end God will destroy all of the forces of evil:

> On that day,
> The LORD will punish with his sword
>   that is cruel, great, and strong,
> Leviathan the fleeing serpent,
>   Leviathan the coiled serpent;
>   and he will slay the dragon that is in the sea. (Isa 27:1)

Israel's stories of creation contain traces of the Near Eastern mythic story, but even these traces have been reinterpreted in ways that demonstrate God's exclusive sovereignty. The stories also reflect the social situations of the people telling the stories. The first account of creation (Gen 1:1–2:4a) begins with four Hebrew words— *tōhû* (formless), *bōhû* (emptiness or wasteland), *ḥōshek* (darkness), and *tᵉhôm* (abyss)—that describe the initial chaos: "the earth was formless wasteland, and darkness covered the abyss" (1:2). There is no cosmic battle—because God has no threatening peers. This creation account does, however, describe a definite ordering. All of the heavenly bodies are assigned their proper places before God calls forth life on the earth.

This first creation account, usually attributed to the Priestly tradition because of its literary style and its insistence on the importance of the Sabbath (Gen 2:3), has a royal character. The man and the woman are made in the image of God (1:27). In the ancient world, this is the way royalty were thought to have been made. Furthermore, they are told to "subdue it [the earth]. Have dominion over the fish . . . the birds . . . and all the living things" (1:28). In the ancient world, this was the responsibility of royalty. In other words, they were to act on earth in God's place. Yet they were only images of God, accountable to God. They sinned when they were not willing to remain subject to God but tried to "be like gods who know what is good and what is bad" (3:5).

The second creation account (Gen 2:4b–3:24) contains no cosmic scene. Even though there are mythic features in this story—trees with wondrous fruits, talking animals, guarding angels—the drama unfolds on earth. The setting of a garden suggests that the story originated among agricultural people. The story itself explains several issues with which the people struggled: Why is there both longing for and tension between women and men? Why is something as natural as childbirth so painful? Why is the ground so difficult to cultivate? (The same Hebrew word describes the pain of childbirth and the toil of cultivation.)

This creation account seems less interested in how things happened in the beginning than in explanations of aspects of life as they experienced them. Still, both accounts underscore certain aspects of biblical faith. In them we see a God who alone is responsible for creation. Though uniquely sovereign, God shares creation with human beings. In the first account, the humans are told to "subdue and have dominion," but with the care that God would show it. In the second account, the man is placed in the garden to "cultivate [the Hebrew word is 'serve'] and care for it" (2:15). The image of God as "creator" is not prominent in the New

Testament. The gospels do depict Jesus as employing nature imagery in many of his parables, but the word "creator" is never used in the gospels and only three times in the entire New Testament.

Familial Images

The relationship between God and the people is sometimes characterized in terms of familial bonds. Though this characterization is not found in early material, it does appear in the poetry of the prophets. In Hosea God refers to Israel as "my son" (Hos 11:1), implying that God was the father. Though not explicitly stated as a male parent, because of the androcentric (male-centered) character of the ancient worldview, God was normally characterized as male. In prayer, Isaiah stated: "You, Lord, are our father" (Isa 63:16). Jeremiah also refers to God as "father" (Jer 3:4, 19; 31:9).

When the New Testament writers have Jesus refer to God as "Father," they have a very different concept in mind than that found in the Old Testament. By the time of the writing of these traditions, the Christian community was beginning to develop a trinitarian understanding of God. Therefore, while these writers are certainly using the image to characterize Jesus' origin from God and the intimate relationship that existed between them, the meaning of the image in the Old Testament, their use of the image implied much more. It pointed to the developing understanding of the relationship between the divine Father and the equally divine Son.

Though there is no passage that explicitly refers to God as "mother," there are instances where God is indirectly described as a mother: "Can a mother forget her infant, / be without tenderness for the child of her womb? / Even should she forget, / I will never forget you" (Isa 49:15); "As a mother comforts her son, / so will I comfort you" (Isa 66:13). "Compassion," the very word that describes God's tenderness toward the people, comes from the Hebrew word for "womb." One might say that God's love for the people is like a woman's love for the child of her womb.

A third familial image of God is that of husband. The prophet Hosea develops this image extensively. In that book, God declares: "She [Israel] shall call me 'My husband'" (Hos 2:18). Jeremiah also employs this image to characterize the intimate relationship existing between God and Israel:

> I [God] remember the devotion of your youth,
>   how you loved me as a bride . . . (Jer 2:2)

The passionate character of this image is found elsewhere in the writings of the same prophet:

> I have loved you with an everlasting love;
>> therefore I have continued my faithfulness to you. (31:3; NRSV)

This image exemplifies both the intimate and the exclusive character of the covenant bond. The declaration, "I will be your God," means I and no one else. In like manner, "You will be my people," means you and no one else. These covenant partners are bound together in intimate and exclusive love.

In the New Testament book of Revelation, the images of bridegroom and bride are employed to characterize the relationship between the Lamb (Christ) and the New Jerusalem, (the church). She is described as "a bride adorned for her husband" (Rev 21:2). This image carries the same meaning as bride/groom does in the Old Testament, namely, intimate and exclusive relationship.

Judge

The image of God as judge, though not a major characterization, is found throughout both testaments of the Bible. This is because of the importance of the notion of justice: when the people were faithful to God, they believed that they would be happy and enjoy peace and prosperity; but if they turned away from God, they expected some form of punishment. The psalms in particular are filled with references to God as judge: "Rise up, judge of the earth" (Ps 94:2). In praising God as judge they are really praising divine justice (Ps 96:13). Other psalms contain a clear prayer for justice. Most likely they originated from a time when the Israelites felt threatened by forces beyond their control and they looked to God for help.

This notion of God as judge takes on a slightly different character when it refers to some form of future judgment. The ancient Israelites initially looked to this time of judgment, called "the Day of the LORD," as that time when retribution would be meted out to its enemies. However, the prophets soon redirected that focus, insisting that Israel itself would face the judgment of God because of its infidelity: "Woe to those who yearn for the day of the LORD! / What will this day of the LORD mean for you? / Darkness and not light!" (Amos 5:18). Reference to this "day of judgment" appears again and again in the New Testament, particularly in Matthew's gospel (Matt 10:15; 11:22, 24; 12:36, 41, 42).

Thus the image of God as judge functions in at least two different yet related ways. First, it underscores belief in divine justice. From this perspective it can function in two major ways: it can instill hope in the hearts of those who are vulnerable and oppressed, and it can function as a deterrent, warning people that retribution will follow offense. Second, this image also reminds women and men of their responsibility to live lives of justice and to work for justice for others. It suggests that if they do not fashion a just society, God will step in and establish it.

Shepherd

One final biblical image of God is found in the writings of the prophet Ezekiel, where God is characterized as shepherd. The image probably originated in the broader ancient Near Eastern world, where many rulers referred to themselves as shepherds of their people. Ezekiel reports that God was unhappy because the rulers of Israel had neglected their responsibilities and had led the people along the wrong path. The rulers had not provided what the people needed to survive and to thrive; they had not cared for the weak and the vulnerable (Ezek 34:1-16). In the face of this, God declares: "I myself will look after and tend my sheep" (34:11). This image captures the solicitude of God in the face of human need. God not only will care for the flock but will face danger if need be in order to protect the people.

Of all of the Old Testament images, that of shepherd is the one chosen by Jesus to identify himself: "I am the good shepherd" (John 10:11). He used it in exactly the same way as Ezekiel used it. This image illustrates the unique loving bond that exists between Jesus and those whom he calls his own: "I know mine and mine know me" (10:14). Jesus also uses this image to underscore the price he is willing to pay to protect those under his care: "I will lay down my life for the sheep" (10:15). Appropriating to himself an image that earlier characterized God might also be seen as a claim of divinity. This may well be the case, since in this passage Jesus speaks of his death and resurrection: "I have power to lay it [my life] down, and power to take it up again" (10:18).

Together, these images of God provide us with some insight into the character of God as sketched in the Bible. God is first and foremost concerned with human well-being. Martin Buber, the great Jewish philosopher, put it succinctly: "God is with us, and God is for us." God can be a reliable protector only because God is sovereign, having no peer and, therefore, no rival. So, if God is for us, there is no comparable power against us. (The question of evil will be treated later.) God is just, establishing order in the world and governing in such a way that that order is either preserved or restored when thwarted. This means that we can trust the forces of life, confident that they are meant to work for our good. Finally, the relationship that God has established is loving and intimate, like that of a father or a mother or a spouse.

Covenant

A covenant is a formal agreement or pact made between two parties as a means of protecting and enhancing the well-being of both parties. The Bible attests to covenants made between individuals and between nations. Some of these covenants were established between equals, while others were between those of unequal social or political status. Examples of the first type include the covenants made by Abram (Abraham) with the Amorites (Gen 14:13) and with Abimelech, the king of Gerar (21:27), the covenant David made with Abner (2 Sam 3:13), and the one between Solomon and Hiram, the king of Tyre (1 Kgs 15:19). These covenants carried mutual responsibilities, which were carefully decided upon before the pact was sealed. Other covenants were made between those who were not equals. This kind of covenant is apparent in the covenant made between the vulnerable Gibeonites and the invading troops of Joshua (Josh 9:6), or between the besieged people of Jabesh-Gilead and their Ammonite attackers (1 Sam 11:2). It is clear that these were covenants made to ensure the protection of the weaker partner. In return the weaker partner promised some form of tribute to their overlord.

This form of political agreement was also used to describe some kind of permanent relationship with God. The Bible recounts several instances of this kind of covenant. In each case, it is God who initiates the covenant and, though it is made through the agency of an individual, the bond established is never solely with that individual.

Noachide

The first appearance of this kind of covenant making is found in the story of the flood (Gen 9). Though made through Noah, this covenant was really made with "all mortal creatures that are on earth" (Gen 9:17). Furthermore, it is said to be an "everlasting covenant" (9:16), implying that chaos will never again be allowed to overwhelm the earth. This flood story had so much in common with the first account of creation (Gen 1:1–2:4a) that scholars soon realized that both stories probably came from the same Priestly tradition. In the first account, creation was brought forth from chaos: "[T]he earth was a formless wasteland and darkness covered the abyss" (1:2); the flood account describes the return of chaos. In these stories, after order was either established or reestablished, God said: "Be fertile, then, and multiply; abound on earth and subdue it" (Gen 9:7, cf. 1:28). The flood story mentions a sign, which points to the major focus of this covenant: "I set my bow in the clouds to serve as a sign of the covenant between me and the earth" (9:13). This is a heavenly or cosmic sign, indicating that the covenant between God and the earth has a cosmic character.

Abrahamic

The second covenant was made with Abram (Abraham). God had just promised Abram that his descendants would be as numerous as the stars in the sky. This promise was then ritualized by a covenant ceremony: "It was on that occasion that the LORD made a covenant with Abram, saying: 'To your descendants I give this land'" (Gen 15:18). There is a second version of a covenant with Abram and promise of descendants and land. In that account, Abram's name was changed to Abraham, which means "the father of a host of nations" (17:5). This second version also includes mention of a sign: "Circumcise the flesh of your foreskin, and that shall be the mark of the covenant between you and me. . . . [M]y covenant shall be in your flesh as an everlasting pact" (17:11, 13). This sign on the flesh of the male genital signified that the covenant was made with the people throughout the generations. It should be noted that it too has an everlasting character.

Mosaic

The covenant that is at the heart of the identity of the people of Israel was the one that God made with them at Sinai through the agency of Moses. It was there that God promised: "Therefore, if you hearken to my voice and keep my covenant, you shall be my special possession, dearer to me than all other people" (Exod 19:5). There are elements in the format of this covenant that resemble a pattern found on tablet remnants of an ancient Canaanite nation known as the Hittites. The covenant described there was between an overlord and vassals. The pattern consisted of six elements: 1) a preamble in which the overlord is identified; 2) a recital of past favors granted by the overlord; 3) a list of the vassal's obligations; 4) a list of the rewards and punishments following obedience or disobedience; 5) a list of the names of witnesses; and 6) provisions for deposit of a record of the covenant and for periodic renewal.

Several elements of this covenant pattern can be found in the account of the Sinai event: "I, the LORD, am your God [preamble], who brought you out of the land of Egypt, that place of slavery [recital of favors]" (Exod 20:2). The Ten Commandments follow, along with an extensive list of laws (20:3-17). Rewards and punishments are found elsewhere in the Bible (Deut 28). Since Israel did not believe in other gods who might stand as witnesses during the making of the covenant, there was no comparable list of names; but when Joshua renewed the covenant after the people had entered the land of promise, a stone was set up as a witness. It symbolized the strength and endurance of the covenant (Josh 24:26-27). Finally, we know that the tablets upon which the Law was inscribed were kept in the ark of the covenant (Exod 25:16) and that Israel did indeed periodically renew the covenant made with God (Josh 24:25). These passages show that the Israelites were acquainted with the Hittite covenant formula and appropriately reshaped it to describe their relationship with their own God.

This Sinai covenant has always been considered the founding covenant with God. By means of it, the Israelites became God's own people and God became their national God: "[Y]ou shall be my special possession, dearer to me than all other people" (Exod 19:5). The Laws, which were part of this covenant, provided the Israelites with direction for living as God's covenant partners. They did not see the Law as burdensome and restricting. Rather, it was "refreshing . . . giving wisdom . . . rejoicing the heart . . . enlightening the eye . . ." (Ps 19:8-9). Though all of the major laws are found in the same place in the Bible (Exodus–Deuteronomy), they probably did not all originate at the same time. Most likely they were simply collected together and placed in the story of the revelation at Sinai. In this way all of Israel's laws, both early and late, were accorded the same Mosaic legitimation.

As with the tradition of the covenant made through Abraham, there is a second important version of the Mosaic covenant: "So shall the Israelites observe the Sabbath, keeping it throughout their generations as a perpetual covenant" (Exod 31:16). This version does not contradict the earlier story; rather, it adds a ritual component to it. Just as the second Abraham version instructed the people to circumcise the men of the community, so this version directs the people to refrain from labor on the Sabbath. The literary character of these second versions and their insistence on the observance of some ritual practice have led scholars to identify them as part of the Priestly tradition. Like the other covenants in this tradition, this covenant is designated as eternal.

The importance of this particular covenant tradition cannot be over-emphasized. It is the foundation of Israel's identity and faith: "I will be your God, and you will be my people" (Lev 26:12). The Law was really a set of guidelines for living out this identity, and the cultic practices contained in the Law celebrated that identity. The message of every prophet was grounded in fidelity to that Sinai covenant. This is true about Amos's insistence on social justice, Hosea's condemnation of cultic perversions, and Jeremiah's charge to accept the conquest by the Babylonians as just punishment for the Israelites' infidelity. This covenant identity also sustained the people during the time of their exile in Babylon, helping them to forge a new understanding of their relationship with God: "The days are coming, says the LORD, when I will make a new covenant with the house of Israel and the house of Judah. . . . I will place my law within them, and write it upon their hearts; I will be their God, and they shall be my people" (Jer 31:31, 33). Their exile helped the people to see what they should always have seen, that fidelity to the covenant meant more than simple external observance. It required a profound interior disposition of commitment.

When the prophets spoke of a new covenant, they were not thinking of a commitment with a different people. They meant the reestablishment of the covenant made through Moses, but now in a new and different way. When the New Testament writers tried to explain how they believed that Jesus was the fulfillment of all of the expectations of ancient Israel, they reshaped this notion of a new covenant, giving it a new meaning without destroying the original meaning. They insisted that a new relationship was established through the death and resurrection of Jesus; and now, those who were baptized into that faith were a new people of God, covenanted with God in a new way. The fact that two religious communities (Jews and Christians) claimed to have a unique covenant relationship with God posed a serious theological problem for Paul. While he taught that Christians were the new covenant community, Paul was not willing to maintain that God had renounced the first community. After all, the tradition claimed that the earlier covenant was everlasting. Just how was this apparent contradiction to be resolved? (Theologians today struggle with the same issue, though the question is no longer, "Are there two covenanted communities?" Instead, the question is, "What is the relationship between the two covenanted communities?")

Just as the covenant with ancient Israel was sealed and confirmed by means of a sacrifice, so the same is true about this new covenant. At the Last Supper, Jesus announced: "This is my blood of the covenant, which will be shed for many" (Mark 14:24; Luke 22:20). It is clear that the early Christian writers were well acquainted with the Israelite covenant traditions, for they based a central segment of their teaching about Jesus on this fundamental theme of Jewish faith.

Davidic

The final covenant tradition is very different from the others. It was made with the house of David:

> Is not my house firm before God?
> He has made an eternal covenant with me. (2 Sam 23:5)

The covenant consisted of a promise made to David that a descendant of his would always reign over the people: "I will raise up your heir after you. . . . I will make his royal throne firm forever. I will be a father to him, and he shall be a son to me" (2 Sam 7:12-14). This is clearly a political covenant that gives the Davidic monarchy divine legitimation. Several hundred years later, when the northern tribes seceded from Davidic rule (1 Kgs 12:16), the southern monarchy would use this theology to condemn the North on charges of infidelity toward God.

Confidence in the "eternal" nature of this covenant resulted in the development of belief in a future royal messiah. The word "messiah" comes from the Hebrew word for "anointed." Since every king was anointed at the time of coronation, every king was, in a sense, a messiah. Over the years, however, disappointment in the actual kings led the people to look to God to send the ideal king:

> The spirit of the LORD shall rest upon him;
> a spirit of wisdom and of understanding,
> A spirit of counsel and of strength,
> a spirit of knowledge and of fear of the LORD,
> and his delight shall be the fear of the LORD. (Isa 11:2-3)

This messianic expectation did not wane with the demise of the Davidic monarchy. In fact, it only grew stronger because of the people's faith in the reliability of God's promises. God had promised that there would always be a Davidic king, and this promise would eventually be kept, because God is faithful.

The New Testament writers saw this Davidic messianic hope fulfilled in Jesus. In their writings, they made many explicit connections between Jesus and David. The New Testament genealogies trace Jesus' ancestry through David (Matt 1:1-17; Luke 3:23-38). Furthermore, he was born in Bethlehem, the city of David (2:5-6). Though Jesus rejected the idea of restoring the kingdom of David as presented to him by his own disciples just before his ascension (Acts 1:6), he allowed people to acclaim him "Son of David" at his triumphant entrance into Jerusalem: "Hosanna to the Son of David" (Matt 21:9). However, the manner of his entry, "meek and riding on an ass" (Matt 21:5) rather than on a magnificent military steed, indicated the self-effacing character of his rule. Jesus may have fulfilled the Davidic expectations, but he it did it in a most unusual manner.

Worship and Prayer

In the Old Testament, the word that we translate "worship" means "to bow down" or "to prostrate oneself." It indicates profound reverence in the presence of the all-holy God. This disposition and manner of behavior was probably patterned after the reverence accorded human sovereigns. The very first commandment obliges Israel to worship God, and only God:

> You shall not have other gods besides me.
> You shall not carve idols for yourselves in the
> shape of anything in the sky above or on the
> earth below or in the waters beneath the earth;
> you shall not bow down before them or worship
> them. For I, the LORD, your God, am a jealous
> God. (Exod 20:3-5; Deut 5:7-9)

The underlying meaning of worship is service. Just as the people were required to serve their human rulers, so service to God was expected of all.

Sacrifice

The primary form of worship in ancient Israel was sacrifice, and a common form of sacrifice was the holocaust or burnt offering (Lev 1). In it, the victim, an unblemished male animal or a bird, was completely burned except for the hide, which went to the priests. This kind of sacrifice signified that the entire victim was given to God. Before the animal was burned, its blood, which represented life, was poured around the altar, indicating that this life really belonged to God. Holocausts were usually offered in order to make atonement for sin or as a thanksgiving offering. This type of sacrifice especially acknowledged the power and might of God. A later law required that flour mixed with oil and a libation of wine be offered along with the holocaust. The flour was burned and the wine poured on the base of the altar.

A second type of bloody sacrifice was the peace offering (Lev 3). It was a kind of communion sacrifice in which only part of the animal was burned. The other parts were roasted and eaten the same day the sacrifice was offered, and were shared by the one offering it and by the officiating priest. Such a ritual was considered a way of eating with the deity. The animal sacrificed here might be a bull or a cow, a sheep or a goat, male or female. A grain offering was part of this sacrifice as well. The peace offering was a celebrative sacrifice offered during communal festivals as well as individual celebrations. It was offered in thanksgiving for God's deliverance, as a votive offering in payment of a vow made in order to secure God's help, or as a simple freewill offering. The Passover sacrifice was this kind of offering.

The New Testament goes to great lengths to show that the sacrifice of Jesus reinterpreted the peace offering that was sacrificed during the feast of Passover. All of the gospels report that Jesus' sacrifice took place during the time of that feast, and his words at the Last Supper imply that his sacrificed body and blood were to be shared by those who partook in the sacrifice. (The meaning of the Passover feast and the New Testament understanding of Jesus as the new Passover will be treated later.)

Ancient Israel offered two other kinds of animal sacrifice: the sin or purification offering (Lev 4:1–5:13), and the guilt or reparation offering (Lev 5:14-26). These were both expiatory sacrifices, offered to make some kind of restitution. Because the biblical passages that describe these two offerings do not clearly distinguish their functions or purposes, scholars differ in their interpretations of them. The victim of the sin offering varied, depending on the status of the one offering the sacrifice. If the offering was expiation for the offenses of either the high priest or the nation as a whole, a bull was offered. On the other hand, a male goat was offered for a member of the royal family and a female goat or sheep for everyone else. Some of the blood of the victim of this sacrifice was rubbed on the altar, the rest of it poured at the altar's base. The fat of the victim was burned, but the flesh was not given to the one for whom the offering was made. The people believed that the sin for which the sacrifice was offered was transferred to the victim. That is why the flesh of the victim was not eaten by the one for whom the sacrifice was offered.

Some scholars maintain that the sin for which this sacrifice was offered was principally an unintentional offense or an act that rendered one ritually impure, such as childbirth or some form of genital discharge. The purification sought in such instances was ritual purification. The guilt offerings, in which the victims were rams, made expiation for a deliberate offense for which one is truly guilty. However these two kinds of offering might be understood, one thing is clear: they were both intended to redress the imbalance created by some infraction. To this end they were believed to effect purification or reparation.

In the New Testament, the sacrifice offered at the purification of Mary (Luke 2:22) was clearly a sin offering, since she was ritually unclean because of childbirth. Joseph and Mary were poor and so they offered a pair of turtledoves or young pigeons as required by law (2:24; Lev 12:6). This example of a sin offering reinforces the purification aspect of that kind of sacrifice, since Mary was certainly not guilty of any deliberate offense. In another New Testament passage, Jesus directs the man cured of leprosy to "go show yourself to the priest, and offer the gift that Moses prescribed" (Matt 8:4). The gift referred to was a peace offering that was required after the man was healed of a disease that had made him ritually unclean (Lev 14:1-9). There is no mention of culpability here, only uncleanness due to disease. The author of the Letter to the Hebrews, on the other hand, interprets the sacrifice of Jesus as the ultimate expiatory ritual of a sin offering enacted by the high priest during the celebration of the Day of Atonement (Heb 9:13-14). These examples show that even into the early Christian era, the sin offering was understood as effecting both purification and reparation for actual sin.

Not all offerings included animal sacrifice. Grain or cereal offerings were made as well. Though the character and purpose of these offerings varied, they were all considered gifts to God. Some offerings required that the cereal be mixed with oil and then burned along with incense, thus producing a sweet-smelling sacrifice. Other offerings were baked before they were burned. Some offerings were completely consumed by the sacrificial flames, while others were shared with the priests.

A very specific kind of sacrifice was that of firstfruits. Each year, the firstfruits of the various harvests and the firstborn of the flocks and herds were offered to God. This ritual was a way of thanking God for the harvest and of acknowledging that all life ultimately belongs to God. At some time in Israel's history, these firstfruits also became a means to support the priests.

Feasts/Festivals

Many of these sacrifices were associated with the major religious feasts. Chief among them were Passover and Unleavened Bread, Weeks or Pentecost, Tabernacles, the Day of Atonement, Hanukkah or Dedication, and Purim. The first three feasts are the oldest and were celebrated as pilgrimage festivals. Though Leviticus clearly mandates the observance of the Day of Atonement (Lev 23:26-32), there is no account in either biblical testament of its observance. Yet it was obviously well known, because the author of the Letter to the Hebrews interprets the sacrifice of Jesus through the lens of the ritual of that day. Hanukkah, which originated in the second century before the Christian era, commemorated the rededication of the temple after Antiochus IV Epiphanes had desecrated it. Like the Day of Atonement, the observance of Purim was mandated (Esth 9:26-32), but there is no narrative that describes or even mentions its observance.

Passover

Passover probably originated as a nomadic ritual practiced to ensure the safety of the flock as it moved from one pasturage to another. Since flocks often traveled in the cool of the night rather than in the heat of the day, the sacrifice of a member of the flock was meant to ward off demons of the night. Such movement usually occurred during springtime. Therefore, the sacrifice might also have been a way to ensure fertility of the flock. This ancient ritual might explain some of the details found in the biblical account of the first Passover sacrifice offered by the people the night before their escape from Egypt (Exod 12:1-30). The original Passover offering was a sacrifice that secured their deliverance; the commemoration of the event, which occurs in springtime, became a weeklong remembrance festival celebrating that deliverance.

The Bible contains several references to the celebration of this festival. The first is the description of the event of deliverance itself (Exod 12). The second reference describes the celebration of the Passover while the people were journeying in the wilderness (Num 9:1-14). Mention of the resident alien (9:14) implied that the people were already established in their own land and ruling over themselves. This suggests that the description of the ritual was a much later account that was read back into the original story of deliverance. Passover was also celebrated just after the people crossed the Jordan River and entered the land of promise (Josh 5:10-12). It seems that this feast was then neglected, for: "No Passover such as this had been observed during the period when the

Judges ruled Israel, or during the entire period of the kings of Israel and the kings of Judah, until the eighteenth year of the king Josiah, when this Passover of the LORD was kept in Jerusalem" (2 Kgs 23:22-23). Finally, Passover was also celebrated by those who had recently returned from exile in Babylon (Ezra 6:19-22).

Each one of the Passover remembrances marks a turning point in the history of the people. The first celebration established the yearly requirement of celebrating the feast: "This day shall be a memorial feast for you, which all your generations shall celebrate with pilgrimage to the LORD, as a perpetual institution" (Exod 12:14). The account of the entrance into the land signified a new phase in the Israelites' existence. Though they could now look forward to a new life in the land that had been promised to their ancestors, they were never to forget that at heart they were people who had been delivered by God. Josiah's reform, which included the injunction of faithful observance of the Passover, was an opportunity for the people to recommit themselves to God.

Unleavened Bread

Unleavened Bread was originally an eight-day agricultural festival that celebrated the spring barley harvest. It seems to have been the primary festival of the people living before the time of the monarchy. Eating bread that was unleavened was a way of refraining from the impurity (fermented yeast) of the previous year. This symbolized purification from the evils of that year. Since both Passover and Unleavened Bread were spring festivals, they were eventually combined. It is difficult to know for sure when this occurred, because the requirement of eating unleavened bread is mentioned in even the earliest accounts of Passover. The feast of Unleavened Bread may have originally been the more significant celebration, but the stories that have come down to us accord that distinction to Passover.

Passover and Unleavened Bread mark some of the most important episodes in the story of Jesus. As a young boy, he went to Jerusalem with his parents to celebrate this festival. It was then that he stayed in the temple, talking with the teachers, and, in a sense, inaugurating his own ministry (Luke 2:41-52). In the Synoptic Gospels (Matthew, Mark, and Luke; so called because of their great similarity), Jesus goes to Jerusalem only once during his ministry, and he goes there to die. The gospels report that it was at the time of Passover and Unleavened Bread (Matt 26:17; Mark 14:12; Luke 22:7). John's gospel reports several visits to Jerusalem, two of which occurred during the time of Passover. The first report describes Jesus' cleansing of the temple (John 2:13-25). John placed this episode at the beginning of Jesus' ministry rather than at the end as did the other gospel writers (Matt 21:12-13; Mark 11:15-18; Luke 19:45-46). Though the miracle at Cana precedes this episode, John's literary arrangement suggests that visits to Jerusalem at the time of Passover frame Jesus' public ministry. In this first visit, Jesus announces: "Destroy this temple and in three days I will raise it up. . . . [H]e was speaking about the temple of his body" (John 2:19, 21). In his last visit (11:55-57), they did indeed destroy the temple of his body; and he did indeed raise it up.

These stories about Jesus' visit to Jerusalem at the time of Passover are told in a way that those who hear or read them will see at once that Jesus is the true Paschal Lamb and that his sacrifice effected true deliverance. Paul used elements from the theology of both Passover and Unleavened Bread in his admonition to the Corinthians to live moral lives: "Clear out the old yeast, so that you may become a fresh batch of dough, inasmuch as you are unleavened. For our paschal lamb, Christ, has been sacrificed. Therefore let us celebrate the feast, not with the old yeast, the yeast of malice and wickedness, but with the unleavened bread of sincerity and truth" (1 Cor 5:7-8).

Pentecost/Weeks

A second pilgrimage festival was the summer feast of Pentecost or Weeks. It was celebrated seven weeks after Unleavened Bread (Deut 16:9), hence the name. It too was an agricultural festival, observed at the time of the wheat harvest. Leavened loaves made from the new wheat were offered during this festival. The meaning and celebration of this feast developed over time. Eventually this simple celebration of harvest came to commemorate the giving of the Law at Sinai. As the feast took on more importance, holocausts, sin offerings, and peace offerings were added to the cereal offerings (Lev 23:18-19).

Though Pentecost was one of the three pilgrimage festivals, it did not compare in importance with Passover or Tabernacles. Some scholars maintain that the unnamed festival mentioned in John 5:1 was this feast of Pentecost, even though there is nothing in the passage itself that might connect it with the feast. It was observance of the Jewish festival of Pentecost that, after the resurrection of Jesus, brought to Jerusalem "Parthians, Medes, and Elamites, inhabitants from Mesopotamia, Judea, and Cappadocia, Pontus and Asia, Phrygia and Pamphylia, Egypt and the districts of Libya near Cyrene, as well as travelers from Rome, both Jews and converts to Judaism, Cretans and Arabs" (Acts 2:9-11). The Pentecost of the Jewish people thus became the occasion for the dynamic experience of the Holy Spirit; this feast of summer harvest became the feast of the harvest of three thousand new converts to the faith (2:41).

Tabernacle/Booths

The third pilgrimage festival was called Tabernacles or Booths. It was so named because the people lived in temporary booths out in the fields and vineyards during the time of autumn harvest. This was obviously the principal harvest and, probably for this reason, the feast was the major feast of the year. As was the case with Pentecost, this harvest celebration eventually took on historical significance. Living in booths reminded the people of their ancestors' sojourn in the wilderness, and so this feast soon commemorated their deliverance. Tradition claims that Solomon dedicated the temple during this festival (1 Kgs 8:2). This added to the importance of that city as the favored place for the celebration of the feast.

According to John's gospel, the third time that Jesus went to Jerusalem was during the time of the feast of Tabernacles (John 7:2). A ceremony conducted on the major day of that festival set the stage for Jesus' words. On that day, the priests took water from the nearby pool of Siloam, processed around the altar seven times, and then poured the water through an opening in the floor onto the ground beneath. This was the context for Jesus' declaration: "Let anyone who thirsts come to me and drink. Whoever believes in me, as scripture says: 'Rivers of living water will flow from within him'" (7:37-38).

According to the same gospel, after spending time on the Mount of Olives, Jesus returned to the temple and made another bold claim: "I am the light of the world. Whoever follows me will not walk in darkness, but will have the light of life" (John 8:12). Perhaps Jesus was moved by the huge golden lamps that stood in one of the outer courts of the temple, lamps that were lighted on the first night of the festival and burned throughout the entire time. In both instances, Jesus' words claim that he fulfills the aspirations associated with this great Jewish feast.

Day of Atonement

An annual ritual of purification and expiation, known as the Day of Atonement, was observed on the final day of the fall festival. At this time, both the sanctuary and the people were purified. The ritual centered around two goats. One was sacrificed as an expiatory offering, and its blood was sprinkled around the sanctuary. The other was brought to the high priest who stretched his hands over the animal, thereby transferring the sins of the people to the goat. This scapegoat was then driven into the desert to die, taking with it the community's guilt (Lev 16:1-22). This ceremony appears to be a combination of two very different rituals: one of purification through the blood of a sacrificed animal (Ezek 43:19-27), the other of transference of guilt (Zech 5:5-11). Though many of the elements of the combined ritual are found in early biblical passages, there is no mention of a specific day set aside for it. Therefore, scholars conclude that it was instituted after the return from exile in Babylon.

The relationship of the blood of Christ to our redemption is emphasized again and again in the early Christian writing. An example can be found in the Letter to the Hebrews. The author used the ritual of the Day of Atonement to explain the efficacy of the death of Jesus (Heb 2:17; 9:11-28). He identified Jesus as the high priest who, by his death rather than his role, enters the holiest section of the temple. There he offers, not the blood of a sacrificed animal, but his own blood to "cleanse our consciences from dead works to worship the living God" (v. 14). In this sacrifice, Jesus is both high priest and victim, offering himself and sealing the new covenant with his own blood. The high priest was required to offer this sacrifice of expiation every year on the Day of Atonement, but, because of the excellence of his victim, Christ offered his sacrifice "once for all" (v. 26).

Hanukkah/Dedication

The feast of Hanukkah or Dedication is sometimes referred to as the feast of Lights. It traces its origin back to the time of the Maccabean revolt in 167 BCE when the Seleucid ruler Antiochus IV Epiphanes desecrated the temple in Jerusalem by setting up a statue of the Greek god Zeus within its precincts. Three years to the day the Jews recaptured the temple and a new altar was dedicated. The celebration lasted for eight days, similar to the observance of the feast of Tabernacles (1 Macc 4:56; 2 Macc 10:6). Since the temple of Solomon was dedicated during the celebration of Tabernacles (1 Kgs 8:2), it seemed right to associate this rededication with that important festival. A legendary story grew up claiming that when the lamps in the temple were lit for the celebration, there was enough oil for only one night. Miraculously, however, the lamps burned throughout the entire eight-day celebration—hence the name, feast of Lights.

The author of the Gospel of John reports that Jesus went to Jerusalem during the feast of Dedication (John 10:22). Though his words on this occasion cannot be linked with the meaning of the feast, it is in the temple during the celebration of its rededication that Jesus reasserts his claim of intimate union with God: "the Father is in me and I am in the Father" (10:38).

The final festival mentioned in the Bible is Purim. Its origin is found in the book of Esther. The setting is the Persian court. The Jewish people once again face certain extermination, but they are saved through the courage of a young Jewish woman named Hadassah (Esther is her Persian name). Placing herself in jeopardy, she intercedes for her people and sets the stage for a plan that will trick the one responsible for their plight. Though the feast celebrates a second deliverance, it contains none of the characteristics of Passover, the celebration of the first deliverance. In fact, it may have been patterned after a Persian festival. There is no trace of this festival in the New Testament.

Psalms

An important part of the sacrifices and festivals through which the people of the Bible demonstrated their loyalty to God was the prayer that accompanied and sometimes described their ritual actions. While expressions of prayer are found throughout the Bible, the best-known prayers are the psalms. The Psalter, the collection of 150 psalms, is really a treasury of ancient Israel's prayer. There are psalms that contain every religious sentiment: psalms of praise (8, 148–150), of lament (51, 137), of trust (4, 91), and of thanksgiving (41, 118). Some psalms reflect Israel's confidence in its monarchy (2, 110); others imply that only the Law is reliable (19, 119). There are liturgical psalms (24) and wisdom psalms (1). There are also psalms that recite the history of the nation from the call of Abraham to the exile in Babylon (78, 135). The variety of psalmic compositions shows that these prayers grew out of every dimension of the life of the people.

In a way, the psalms are a composite of the major theology of the Old Testament. They address God as deliverer (106), creator (8), warrior (24), judge (7), father (68), and shepherd (23). They praise God for the covenants made through Abraham (105), through Moses (25), and through David (98), and they call the people to be faithful to these covenants. Though the psalms are prayers to God, they reveal the traits of human beings, both their strengths and their weaknesses. At times they demonstrate profound trust in God; at other times they reveal shocking disregard for other nations. They are a microcosm of the reality of ancient Israel.

Since most of the New Testament writers had Jewish roots, they were quite familiar with the psalms. They frequently reinterpreted passages from these prayers to demonstrate some aspect of their faith in Jesus. For example, the words of praise the people shouted as Jesus entered the city of Jerusalem—"Blessed is he who comes in the name of the Lord" (Matt 21:9; Mark 11:9; Luke 19:38)—were taken from Psalm 118:26. Jesus' cry of agony on the cross—"My God, my God, why have you forsaken me?" (Matt 27:46; Mark 15:34)—comes from Psalm 22:2. When Jesus denounced the leaders of the people with the words, "The stone that the builders rejected, / has become the cornerstone" (Matt 21:42; Mark 12:10; Luke 20:17), he was quoting Psalm 118:22. The prayer Mary recited after Elizabeth recognized the identity of the child that Mary was carrying in her womb (Luke 1:46-55) was inspired by Hannah's prayer when she offered her son Samuel to God (1 Sam 2:1-10). Finally, Paul constantly weaves references from the psalms into his teaching, for, as stated above, the psalms are not only prayers; they are also statements of faith.

Summary

At the heart of biblical religion is the conviction that God has initiated a loving relationship with human beings. All of the religious beliefs and practices that we find in the Bible are human responses to that relationship. Regardless of what the people experienced in life, they believed that God was with them and wanted what was best for them. Thus, when they were threatened by enemies, they envisioned God as a mighty warrior fighting for them; when they were disconsolate, they perceived God as a tender mother consoling them. Their perceptions of God sprang from a combination of their belief that God was there for them and their immediate need. The images of God and the religious practices that they developed all reflect the culture of the times. Once again we see how important it is to understand the cultures and customs of the day in order to grasp their authentic religious meaning.

Chapter 4

From God

It may appear to some that the Bible is simply a collection of the stories and laws of ancient people that developed out of history, in a place, and about God. This is certainly not the case. Both the ancient Israelites and the early Christians, from whom the Bible originated, believed not only that their traditions were about God but that they actually came *from* God. This is particularly clear in the writings of the prophets where again and again we find the expression: "Thus says the LORD." This indicates that the words spoken by the prophets are really the words of God.

The Old Testament shows that at times Israel did indeed resort to techniques of divination, which is an attempt to discover future events or hidden knowledge: Joseph interpreted dreams (Gen 37:5-11; 41:25-32), Jonathan used the position of arrows to discover if David's life was in jeopardy (1 Sam 20:35-39), King Saul even had a medium conjure up the ghost of Samuel who foretold the king's demise (1 Sam 28:8-11). As impressive as such instances might have been, none of them included genuine prophetic revelation. The real prophets were less interested in the future than in the present. Grounded in covenant theology, they called the people back to fidelity when they had strayed from their commitments, and they also encouraged them to remain faithful when they may have been tempted to give up. It was only because the prophets believed that God would eventually reward loyalty or punish disloyalty that they spoke of the future. One might say that they were rooted in past covenant theology, committed to present devotion, and aware of future consequences.

The New Testament also claims that the Bible comes from God. It consistently affirms the revelatory character of the message of the prophets as it speaks of the mystery that unfolded in the life of Jesus, from his birth in Bethlehem (Matt 2:5-6) to his death in Jerusalem (Luke 18:31). Though at times the gospel writers changed ever so slightly the original meaning of the prophetic message so that it would better fit their experience and interpretation of Jesus, they nonetheless turned to the prophets because they considered their messages as the word of God. Yet it was not only the Old Testament that they considered the word of God. Some of the New Testament writers clearly placed their own teaching in that category. Paul is an example of this. He claimed that his teaching about Jesus was as revelatory as was the teaching of the prophets: ". . . in receiving the word of God from hearing us, you received not a human word but, as it truly is, the word of God, which is now at work in you who believe" (1 Thess 2:13). In writing to his disciple Timothy, Paul insisted: "All scripture is inspired by God and is useful for teaching, for refutation, for correction, and for training in righteousness" (2 Tim 3:16).

Revelation

Revelation is that which is "uncovered" or "disclosed." It refers to something that is true, but it has been previously concealed or unknown. Revelation is not knowledge that we can come to by ourselves; it must be made known to us by another. Human beings can, of course, reveal information to another, but only God can reveal the fundamental truths about God. The Bible claims that it is revelation from God. But what is the content of that revelation? We have already seen that biblical faith was not some form of supernatural revelation that supposedly came directly from heaven, having nothing at all to do with earth. Rather, it was precisely within the context of the actual life experience of believers that revelation unfolded for them. And what was the content of this revelation? It was the self-revelation of God. In other words, God was self-revealing in the events of history.

We find divine self-revelation from the earliest chapters of the Bible: "Fear not, Abram! / I am your shield" (Gen 15:1); "I am the LORD who brought you from Ur of the Chaldeans" (15:7). God also reveals to Isaac: "I am the God of your father Abraham" (26:24); to Jacob: "I, the LORD, am the God of your forefather Abraham and the God of Isaac" (28:13); and then to Moses: "I am the God of your father . . . the God of Abraham, the God of Isaac, the God of Jacob" (Exod 3:6). Passages such as these show a personal God who identifies with people. In support of this, it was God who declared, "I will take you as my own people, and you shall have me as your God" (Exod 6:7; Lev 26:12; Jer 7:23; 30:22; Ezek 36:28).

In the New Testament, this personal character of God is captured in various ways. There, God is not only Father of Jesus but Father to the disciples as well: "Be merciful, just as [also] your Father is merciful" (Luke 6:36). Jesus even teaches his disciples to pray to God as Father: "Our Father in heaven . . ." (Matt 6:9; Luke 11:2). The relationship between Jesus and his disciples is also intimate. In fact, he shares with them some of the fruits of his relationship with his Father: "I have called you friends, because I have told you everything I have heard from my Father" (John 15:15).

Other characteristics of God are revealed in various places of the Bible: "I have witnessed the affliction of my people in Egypt. . . . I have come down to rescue them. . . ." (Exod 3:7-8); "I will raise up your [David's] heir after you . . . and I will make his [Solomon's] kingdom firm" (2 Sam 7:12); "I will gather you from the nations and assemble you from the countries over which you have been scattered" (Ezek 11:17). These and other similar passages trace the concern that God had for the people of Israel through their entire history. This same concern for the needs of the people is found in the New Testament where Jesus assures his disciples: "Your Father knows what you need before you ask him" (Matt 6:8; Luke 12:30). Such concern should not surprise us, for both testaments bear witness to God's love: "I have loved you with an everlasting love" (Jer 31:3, NRSV); "For God so loved the world that he gave his only son" (John 3:16).

These passages clearly show that the content of biblical revelation is actually divine self-revelation. It is in Scripture that we find characteristics of God and evidence of God's gracious care. The Bible does not contain carefully designed theological statements of doctrine. Such statements developed much later out of reflection on the elements of biblical revelation. What we do find in Scripture are hints of how God can be known through the marvels of creation and in the events of life.

One might say that the Bible is a record of God's self-revelation to select groups of people in both testaments. These people were chosen to make this God known to the rest of the world: ". . . among the nations make known his deeds" (Isa 12:4); ". . . you will be my witnesses in Jerusalem, throughout Judea and Samaria, and to the ends of the earth" (Acts 1:8). The laws and exhortations found throughout the Bible are really instructions that direct those chosen people in right living. The stories describe how they were sometimes faithful to their call and at other times unfaithful. This religious tradition, though, was not merely for people in the past. Its message is for people in the present and future as well. As Paul stated: "All scripture is inspired by God and is useful for teaching, for refutation, for correction, and for training in righteousness" (2 Tim 3:16).

Inspiration

When we say that Scripture is inspired, we mean that it was under the influence of the Spirit of God. This influence was not limited to those after whom the books of the Bible were named. Rather, the Bible was shaped and handed down, and it continues to be handed down under the influence of that Spirit today. Perhaps the best example of the influence of the Spirit is found in the accounts of the call of the prophets: "The spirit of the Lord GOD is upon me" (Isa 61:1); "the spirit of the LORD fell upon me" (Ezek 11:5). The prophet Joel announced:

> Then afterward I will pour out
>   my spirit on all mankind.
> Your sons and daughters shall prophecy,
>   your old men shall dream dreams,
>   your young men shall see visions;
> Even on the servants and the handmaids,
>   in those days, I will pour out my spirit. (Joel 3:1-2)

This is a remarkable promise. It implies that some day all believers will be filled with the Spirit of God. The New Testament author of the Acts of the Apostles claims that the "afterward" referred to by the prophet was the time of fulfillment that dawned with the coming of Jesus and was brought to completion on Pentecost by the Holy Spirit (Acts 2:16-17).

If Paul was correct that "[a]ll scripture is inspired," then even the stories of the escape from Egypt, the laws given at Sinai, the accounts of the institution of the monarchy, the narrative of the passion and death of Jesus, and the instructions found in the New Testament epistles are somehow inspired. Scholars today maintain that the Spirit of God was involved in the entire process of tradition development. This means that those who first told how God had acted in their lives were influenced by the Spirit, but so were those who handed that story down from generation to generation, and those who finally put it in the form that has come down to us.

Understanding inspiration in this way should help us to see how the Bible is said to be inspired for us today. Inspiration is not somehow captured in the Bible, our task being to discover it and release it. Rather, we believe that the Spirit of God is active in the church, just as that Spirit was active in earlier communities of believers. We read that Jesus promised this Spirit: "The Advocate, the holy Spirit that the Father will send in my name—he will teach you everything and remind you of all that [I] told you" (John 14:26). Later in that same gospel we read that on the evening of the resurrection Jesus "breathed on them and said to them, 'Receive the holy Spirit'" (20:22). Now the Spirit lives in all believers: "Do you not know that you are the temple of God, and that the Spirit of God dwells in you?" (1 Cor 3:16). It is the Spirit within us, within the community, that guides the church in its interpretation of Scriptures.

"Fulfilled in your hearing"

In the Gospel according to Luke, the testimony of Jesus' public ministry opens with an account of his teaching in the synagogue in Nazareth, his hometown. There we read that Jesus appropriated to himself the promises found in two passages from the prophet Isaiah:

> The Spirit of the Lord is upon me,
>   because he has anointed me to bring glad tidings to the poor.
> He has sent me to proclaim liberty to captives
>   and recovery of sight to the blind, to let the oppressed go free,
> and to proclaim a year acceptable to the Lord.
>   (Luke 4:18-19; see Isa 61:1-2; 58:6)

The words probably originally referred to one of the Israelite leaders who, after the exile, was expected to establish a community that was totally committed to God and sensitive to the needs of the most vulnerable members of society. This passage looked forward to the jubilee year, the "year acceptable to the Lord," when all debts would be forgiven and the people would be able to start all over again. The people believed that in this way the nation of Israel would be rejuvenated.

When Jesus declared that these promises were fulfilled in the hearing of his audience, he was redirecting their meaning to himself. More than redirecting, he was reinterpreting them as well. First, the people originally looked forward to the reestablishment of a particular sociopolitical religious group. However, the people that Jesus would fashion would not be limited to one social, political, or religious group. It was to be a group accessible to everyone. Second, contrary to the expectations of even religious people, Jesus would not choose a political approach to accomplish his plan. His way would be the way of service.

We can see from this that what may have been basically the same set of promises had very different meanings in different situations. Hence we cannot expect a rigid literal reading of the Bible to open us to its full revelatory value. The working of the Holy Spirit in each successive community of believers opens the message of the Bible in new and profound ways. The Spirit is ever working to provide us with new insights into the ways of God. Careful interpretation of the Bible is necessary if we are to discover what it may have to say to us today. (Various methods of interpretation will be covered in chapter 8.)

Summary

The Bible is considered the foremost authority on religious matters because it is inspired by God and it contains examples of divine self-revelation. Being the foremost authority does not mean, however, that it is the only authority. Catholics also revere authentic tradition as an ongoing source of revelation. This tradition refers to both the content and the dynamic of religious insights and beliefs, worship and practice that originated and grew out of ongoing interpretation and reinterpretation of the truths found in the Bible. These truths may be constant, but their expression often changes with changing circumstances. In this way, the message of the Bible is always the same yet ever new.

Part II

What Did It Mean?

The first task of an introduction to the Bible is informational, telling the reader what the Bible says. It does not take long, though, before that same reader asks: But what does it mean? Such a question might spring from the unfamiliarity of many of the persons, places, and practices of the women and men found within the pages of the Bible. That question is usually asking for more than simple information. Why did the biblical people say what they said, and why did they do what they did? If, as we have seen, the Bible is about God, we want to know what these people thought about God and why they thought what they did. Furthermore, if the Bible is more than a record of the faith of ancient peoples, as we believe it is, and if its message speaks to believers of all ages, as we believe it does, then that initial question takes a new form: What does it mean for us today? We are now faced with two different questions: What *did* the Bible mean to the ancient people? What *does* it mean to us today? The first question will be addressed in this second part of the book. The second question will be dealt with in the third part.

From the beginning, believers have known that at times their religious traditions meant exactly what they said, and at other times they meant more than what they said. That was the case because people have always expressed themselves in many different ways. For instance, when we say "I almost died in that accident," we expect people to take our words literally, which is not the case when we say, "I almost died laughing." Then our words have a more-than-literal meaning. As we grow up in our particular cultures, we learn which sayings are to be taken literally and which are not. Since the Bible comes from cultures very different from our own, it is often quite difficult for us to know which way of understanding is appropriate. This is why interpretation is so important.

Chapter 5

What Kind of Book Is It?

The first part of this book has already addressed the historical dimension of the Bible. There we saw the role that actual historical events played in the development of the various traditions. As important as historical details may be for our grasp of the biblical content, the Bible itself is not a book of history. Rather, history is the matrix out of which the Bible's various traditions sprang and the context within which they are interpreted. History is the stage on which the drama unfolds; it is not the drama itself. Theology reveals that drama! The importance of the complex relationship between theology and history cannot be denied. In fact, that relationship is well captured in the phrase already discussed in the introduction of this book: "The Bible is the word of God in human words."

Literary Forms

In order to discover the theological or religious meaning of the Bible we must first understand its manner of expression. Is it prose, or is it poetry? Is it fact, or is it legend? Is it advice, or is it a command? For example, we know that poetry is not factual in the way we expect various forms of prose to be. Poetry is more like a collage of images, one image next to or on top of or within another. Poetry creates a perception of some aspect of reality rather than a definition of it. Prose, on the other hand, is more precise than it is metaphorical. It is more interested in data and facts than in impressions. Both prose and poetry express truth, but they do so in very different ways.

Like poetry, legends are imaginative creations rather than exact descriptions. They are heroic stories about actual historical people of the past, but some of the events and the details of the stories may not be historically accurate. Legends are characterized by exaggeration intended to make a particular point, while fact is more precise and seeks to avoid exaggeration. Finally, though at times they may be expressing the same idea, advice and command differ considerably. Strictly speaking, we are free to accept or reject advice: "I wouldn't do that if I were you." However, we are obliged to follow a command: "You may not do that."

People express themselves in different ways, and as we grow up in or become acquainted with a particular culture, we learn how to understand those expressions. When we consider these questions in our study of the Bible, we are acknowledging that the Bible is literature. Actually, it is a collection of several very different kinds of literary works. This in no way diminishes its identity as a religious testimony and a theological document. It simply means that this theology has come down to us in various literary forms or genres. It also means that we must understand the literary forms if we are to understand the message conveyed by means of them.

As we move through the pages of the Bible, we discover some distinctive literary forms. The first twelve chapters of the book of Genesis consist of stories of extraordinary events and of people possessing superhuman characteristics. It is there that we find two versions of the creation of the world and of humankind within it. A careful reading of these stories will show that they do not pretend to be history or science: light is created before any luminary that might emit the light (Gen 1:3), people converse with serpents (3:1-5), heavenly creatures mate with human women (6:2), people live for 960 years (5:27), boats are constructed that can hold a menagerie of animals (6:19-20; 7:2-3). Such stories belong to the category of myth.

Myths are stories about superhuman characters or amazing events that occur in otherworldly time and space. They employ symbolic language to explain or demonstrate transcendent reality. They often describe fundamental issues, creation, suffering, murder, progress, and relationship with God, to name but a few. Myths are usually culture-specific, using details from the lives of the people concerned. This explains why a second culture may not understand the symbolism of a particular myth and, therefore, the profound meaning behind it. It has been said that myths deal with aspects of reality too basic to life or too important to a people for mere history or science to describe. History and science may be precise, but they are too specific to embrace many of the most profound facets of reality. History, science, and myth all deal with truth, but they deal with it in different ways.

It is not until the twelfth chapter of Genesis that the biblical narratives take on the character of history. Beginning with the traditions about the ancestors (Abraham and Sarah, Isaac and Rebekah, Jacob, Leah, and Rachel) through the accounts of the exodus from Egypt and the entrance into the land of promise, to the reports of the nation first under the monarchy and then occupied by various nations, the biblical stories unfold like a kind of history. Even then, that history, as all history, is told from a particular point of view. In those stories we detect ethnocentric bias in the way all of the political moves made by the Israelites are justified; we perceive elements of the social structure of the people in the character of the laws that they observed; we become aware of their religious worldview in the way they describe their worship. While much of what we find in these stories may reflect the general culture of the ancient Near Eastern world, the dissimilarities that we discover between that world and the world of the Israelites provide us with a sketch of what is uniquely Israelite.

The role played by the nation's religious and political point of view in interpreting the events and people of its time can be clearly seen in the books of Chronicles. These books report events already recorded in the earlier books of Samuel and Kings. This similarity may explain why people generally turn to the earlier version of the story found in Samuel and Kings rather than the reinterpreted version in Chronicles. The later version, however, is quite different. In many places it expands the original story, adding list upon list of names of temple personnel. In other places it adds details that shift the original perspective, sometimes substantially, sometimes ever so slightly. For instance, it is in Chronicles that we find that, despite his desire to build the temple, David was prevented from doing so, because he was responsible for so much bloodshed (1 Chr 28:3). This shows us that after the exile, when Chronicles was written, Israel had a very different perspective on David's character.

Even within these quasi-historical stories we find examples of other kinds of narrative. There are ancestral legends like the story of Jacob wrestling with an angel (Gen 32:23-33), directives for the celebration of various feasts like Passover (Exod 12:1-28) or Purim (Esth 9:20-32), sagas or hero stories like the exploits of Samson (Judg 13–16), and court documents that record information about the monarchy (1 Kgs 12–16). There are stories that give religious legitimation (justifying them as having been directed by God) to battles (Josh 3:10), to the establishment of the monarchy (1 Sam 8:9) and the Davidic dynasty (2 Sam 7:16), and to court intrigue (1 Kgs 1:30). Finally, sprinkled throughout this large complex of narratives are short stories. Within the book of Genesis we find a collection of accounts about Joseph (Gen 37–48). There are also short books that are set in history, but which are really short novels: Ruth, Tobit, Esther, and Judith.

While narrative might be the basic literary form of a passage, that passage usually contains many other forms as well. For example, the story of the escape from bondage in Egypt includes an extensive collection of laws. In fact, the major content of four biblical books (Exodus, Leviticus, Numbers, and Deuteronomy) is largely some form of law. There are genealogies that trace descent (Gen 11:10-32), census records used for purposes of taxation (Ezra 2:3-63), lists of names of conquered kings (Josh 12:1-24), hymns of praise that celebrate victory (Exod 15:1-17; Judg 5:1-31) or extol God's favors received (1 Sam 2:1-10), and elegies that mourn fallen heroes (2 Sam 1:19-27). There are also parables (2 Sam 12:1-6) and riddles (Judg 14:14-18). The biblical narratives are replete with various literary forms.

The biblical story of Israel leads us from the period of the early ancestors (ca. 2000 BCE) to the end of the Maccabean revolt (ca. 160 BCE). The books that contain this story comprise two major collections referred to as the Pentateuch, from the Greek word for "five," and the Historical Books. These collections are followed by another collection known as the Wisdom Literature. In several ways, this is a distinctly different kind of literature. Most obviously, it is not narrative; it does not have a storyline. This literature is written in poetic form rather than prose. Furthermore, it is not interested in specific events, whether historical or mythic. Wisdom literature is interested in the realities of life in general. It deals with human behavior, human accomplishments, and human misfortune.

The primary wisdom form is the proverb. It is a short, pithy saying that describes life experience:

> The words of the wicked are a deadly ambush,
>   but the speech of the upright saves them. (Prov 12:6)

Each proverb is like a snapshot, catching some aspect of life. While it is clearly descriptive, it is meant to encourage a certain kind of behavior. One might say that the proverb describes how life works, and it is up to the person to live in accord with the order found in that description.

Those who have learned from life experience are considered wise, while those who have not learned are thought to be foolish. Though wisdom teaching is really advice, there is a moral dimension to it as well. The wise person will choose the way of righteousness, while the fool will fall into sinful ways.

Since wisdom teaching is concerned with correct behavior, it can be considered instructional. Here the person with experience provides guidance or direction to the uninformed:

> Hear, my son, your father's instruction,
>   and reject not your mother's teaching. (Prov 1:8)

Besides the proverb, various literary forms aid in this instruction. Chief among them are the parable, the riddle, the admonition, and narrative reflections on life. The parable and the riddle contain hidden meanings that challenge people to think, and the admonition provides counsel. Every culture has its wisdom teaching; but because the wisdom perspective is not culture-specific, very little cultural difference is reflected in the wisdom sayings of different people. This shows that many proverbs address aspects of life that are universally applicable.

While wisdom forms and wisdom teaching can be found throughout the Bible, some books have been specifically designated as wisdom teaching. The book of Job consists of a framing prose folktale that sets the stage for a poetic unfolding of the drama of a man struggling with the problem of the suffering of the innocent. The book of Ecclesiastes, consisting of both prose and poetic descriptions, tells of a man searching for meaning in life. Sirach (Ecclesiasticus) and the Wisdom of Solomon also contain wisdom teaching in poetic form. Some scholars include in this category the Song of Songs, which is a collection of erotic love poetry.

Another collection of writings that are poetic in form is the Prophetic Literature. While each book in this collection contains some narrative material describing the historical situation within which the prophet lived, the prophetic words themselves are in a distinct poetic form known as the oracle. The oracle usually begins with words like: "Thus says the LORD." This phrase indicates that the message that follows comes to the people from God.

There are basically two kinds of oracles, the oracle of salvation and the woe-oracle or oracle of doom. The oracle of salvation contains words of hope and comfort: "Comfort, give comfort to my people, says your God" (Isa 40:1). This message is proclaimed to the people when they are in serious distress and on the verge of giving up hope. The oracle of doom condemns them for their betrayal of the covenant bond that unites them with God: "Woe to them, they have strayed from me!" (Hos 7:13). While both of these oracles focus the people's attention on their present life, they each also hint at the consequences that would follow their response to the prophetic word. The people to whom Isaiah's words of comfort were originally addressed were reassured and, presumably, stepped back from despair. The woe addressed to the people at the time of Hosea contained a warning of impending disaster because of their unfaithfulness.

One biblical book does not fit comfortably in any of the blocks of literature already described. That is the book of Psalms. Some commentators classify it with the Wisdom Literature. Although there are psalms that have been identified as wisdom psalms, the book itself is really not a book of instruction. It is a collection of religious songs or prayers. A close look at this book will show that it is actually a collection of collections. Some of the individual psalms come from a collection identified as the psalms of David (Ps 86), others from the psalms of Korah (Ps 44), or the psalms of Asaph (Ps 74). There even seems to have been a collection attributed to Solomon (Ps 72). As the book stands today, the psalms have been divided into five books, each ending with a doxology or prayer of praise (Pss 41:14; 72:18-19; 89:53; 106:48; and the entire Ps 150). This division into five books, reminiscent of the five books of the Pentateuch and the fact that the first psalm is a wisdom psalm have led some to conclude that the book of Psalms was at times used for instruction. This might well have been the case, since all of the major theology of Israel can be found in these religious prayers. This might also explain the inclusion of the book in the Wisdom Literature.

As religious songs or prayers, the psalms express the religious sentiments of the ancient Israelites, sentiments that sprang from the ups and downs of life experience. There are hymns of praise, extolling God for the wonders of the natural world (Ps 8) and for the extraordinary blessings that God bestowed upon the people (Ps 33). A particular type of hymn of praise is called the enthronement psalm, because it praises God who is enthroned in the heavens. There are laments that cry out from the midst of suffering, complaining to God about some affliction, and begging that that affliction be removed. Some of the laments are meant for the personal prayer of an individual (Ps 51); others, for the prayer of the community. About one-third of the entire collection of psalms consists of laments, most of which are prayers of individuals.

Closely associated with the laments are the psalms of trust. They express confidence that God will indeed relieve those who suffer. Like the laments, there are both individual and communal prayers of trust. There are also psalms of thanksgiving that express Israel's gratitude to God for having been heard. Here too there are individual and communal prayers of thanksgiving. Some scholars believe that originally the lament may have had three movements: the lament proper, which cries out in grief; a prayer of confidence that God will hear the lament; and a prayer of thanking God in advance, because the petitioner is convinced that the prayer for help will be heard.

Though these are the primary categories of psalms, other types as well are included. Royal or messianic psalms either acclaim the king himself (Ps 110) or the special covenant that God established with the Davidic family (Ps 89). Some psalms are called songs of Zion because they extol the city of Jerusalem (Ps 46). The wisdom psalms do not even seem to be directed explicitly toward God. Rather, they contain instruction on proper behavior (Ps 1). There are psalms that have a definite liturgical character (Ps 24), while others recount the marvelous deeds of God in the history of the people (Ps 78). Every aspect of Israel's life is reflected in these prayers, because Israel believed that God was somehow present and active in every aspect of life.

As we move into the New Testament, the first books we encounter are the four gospels. The word "gospel" comes from the Old English word meaning "good word." It is a translation of the Greek word for "good news." Gospel is actually used in two ways. It refers primarily to the fundamental proclamation of faith, to the message itself. And what is this basic message? It is: "Jesus is Lord!" Only secondarily does gospel refer to the narrative form that that preaching finally took. When Paul talks about the gospel (Gal 1:7), he is referring to the message of his preaching, not to any book. The gospel credited to Mark is the only one of the canonical gospels that identifies the writing that follows as a gospel: "The beginning of the gospel of Jesus Christ [the Son of God]" (Mark 1:1).

Most people are acquainted with the four canonical or official gospels: Matthew, Mark, Luke, and John. Yet several other pieces of ancient literature have also been classified as gospels: the Gospel of Thomas is a collection of sayings attributed to Jesus, the Gospel of Peter was a popular early Christian version of the passion of Jesus, the Gospel of Mary Magdalene describes Mary's encouragement of the other disciples after the resurrection, the newly rediscovered Gospel of Judas claims that that disciple's betrayal was done in accordance with secret instructions received from Jesus. For various reasons, the early church rejected these documents as genuine gospels. Yet they continue to be important as apocryphal or "set aside" literature. They are set aside, or not included in the list of official books, because they do not contain teaching about Jesus that was faithful to the early church's self-understanding. At the same time, they are valuable because they throw light on how some Christians at various times in history understood the gospel proclamation.

If we begin with the fundamental proclamation that "Jesus is Lord!" we may then say that each gospel proclaims this message in its own unique way. Depending on the audience that will first hear and later read this Good News, the respective gospel reaches into the ancient Jewish tradition to explain the meaning of Jesus' life, death, and resurrection, and it develops this meaning in a narrative form. Though the gospel appears to be a "life of Jesus," it is really an unfolding of the meaning of the proclamation, "Jesus is Lord!" All of the stories that make up this narrative form serve the same purpose: they highlight some aspect of this gospel proclamation.

A second long narrative, the Acts of the Apostles, follows the four gospels. Aspects of both its plot and its literary style have led scholars today to consider it the second of a two-volume work associated with one of the gospels and known as Luke-Acts. The book of Acts of the Apostles is an example of ancient historical writing. It may be divided into two discrete parts: the Acts of Peter, which trace the development of the early community under the leadership of Peter; and the Acts of Paul, which move this development out of Jewish circles into the Gentile world.

A series of epistles follows the Acts of the Apostles. Though these epistles are sometimes called letters, some scholars distinguish between the two forms. A letter is a form of communication between individuals. It is usually private in nature. An epistle, though it is written in the style of a letter, is a carefully constructed literary composition meant to influence the public in some way. It is more than informational; it is instructive or polemical. The public nature of the New Testament epistles or letters can be seen in the fact that they are addressed to: "the beloved of God in Rome" (Rom 1:7), "the church of God that is in Corinth" (1 Cor 1:2; 2 Cor 1:1), "the church of the Thessalonians" (1 Thess 1:1; 2 Thess 1:1), and so forth. Though there are letters that were written to individuals such as Timothy, Titus, and Philemon, these letters were concerned with matters facing not only a designated local community but the entire church.

The last book of the Bible, the book of Revelation, is a unique form of literature. It is an apocalypse (from the Greek verb for "to uncover" or "to reveal"), a narrative account of a human being's reception of a revelation from some heavenly being. It presumes an ancient belief that before time as we know it began, secrets of the future were written in a book that was then sealed to be opened at the end of time. The apocalypse is the account of the uncovering of those secrets. Yet the coded symbolic language of the revelation continues to hide the meaning of the secrets from all but those who know the code. This form of literature arose at times of great distress: the Old Testament book Daniel, during the Seleucid persecution of the Jews; Revelation, during the Roman persecution of the Christians. Despite its descriptions of suffering, the apocalypse always ends with good conquering evil. Thus, though it reports great affliction, its message is really one of hope.

The Canon

We have already seen that the formation and development of the many and varied traditions that ultimately made up the Bible have a long and complicated history. We have seen that there is sometimes more than one version of the same story; there are two very different creation narratives and four distinct gospels. We have also come to know that there are several writings that originated at the same time as some of the biblical writings, but were not incorporated with them. Examples of these include 1 Esdras, A Letter of Jeremiah, the Gospel of Thomas, and the Gospel of Mary. This makes us wonder: What determined which books were considered inspired? And who made that determination?

From the fourth century CE, the word "canon" has been used to designate the official list of biblical books. Originally meaning "reed," canon came to signify something that acted as a measuring reed or stick, a norm or standard. In this context, it refers to those biblical traditions that are the root within statements about the self-understanding of the ancient Israelites and/or the early Christians. These statements define these people as they perceive themselves, and they also direct the further development of that self-understanding.

The process of canonization, or determining the standard for understanding and judging, began as far back in history as the time of the judges, when the ancient Israelites first described orally and eventually in written form how they understood God's activity in their lives. These are the traditions that were handed down generation after generation, as new traditions developed out of that same point of view. We are quite certain that not all of the religious tradition has survived. It is clear that among those that have survived, not all enjoy the same degree of importance and authoritativeness.

Prominent people within the community made the ultimate decisions about inclusion of the tradition; but these people did not simply create religious understandings or teachings as if independent of the broader community. Some of these people may have possessed unique creative insights, such as the prophets or sages, but whatever they brought forth had to be recognized by the community as an authentic expression of their communal understanding. We can conclude from this that a variety of forces were at work shaping and reshaping the religious consciousness and self-understanding of the people. In other words, there was no single locus of origin or of authority. Some individuals and groups originated the traditions; others contributed to their development and reshaping; still others were involved in determining their place and significance in the community's self-understanding. Those in leadership positions may have authenticated the traditions, but it was the people who had to confirm their decisions.

One of the major characteristics of this process of tradition development and ultimate canonization was the community's ongoing reinterpreting of earlier traditions. The people did not merely hand their traditions down to the next generation. They reshaped them in the process of transmission. Changes in social, political, or religious understandings required new expressions of fundamental faith as well as the articulation of new insights. The interaction between historical events and various forces within the historical community determined the shape of the tradition, a shape that might change at another time or in another place.

This process of change and development might have continued to the present day had not several significant events compelled the community to endorse some statements over others and to confer authority on those chosen. As we have seen, the sociopolitical move from a federation of loosely knit tribes to a nation under the administration of a king (ca. tenth century BCE) was one such period; the split of the kingdom into two independent kingdoms (922 BCE) was another; the fall of the northern kingdom to Assyrian forces (722 BCE) was yet another. The exile in Babylon (587–538 BCE) was probably the most significant of these determining events in the history of the people of Israel.

As we move to the New Testament we see that the event of Christ impacted those who believed in him not unlike that of other revelatory events in the history of the People of God. The Christ event forced believers to examine their beliefs in a new way. In order to understand Jesus, they reached into their rich Jewish religious tradition and interpreted Jesus from the point of view of some of those traditions. In doing so, they also reinterpreted the earlier Jewish tradition. A second historical watershed that played a significant role in the decisions regarding the canon of the New Testament was the Roman destruction of the Herodian temple at the time of the emergence of early Christianity (70 CE). It forced a new perspective and it engendered new insights.

Three major Jewish theories address the closing of the Jewish canon. Most of the religious traditions were in existence by the time of Ezra in the fifth century BCE. Ezra himself is thought to be the one who made the final decision. This would explain why books written after this time, such as Sirach and the Wisdom of Solomon, are not included in the Jewish listing. This tradition is legendary and very few people hold it today. A second theory maintains that a group of leaders in the post-exilic community, forerunners of what came to be known as the Great Synagogue, worked under the direction of Ezra, and they determined the official listing. Since there is no evidence that a body resembling the Great Synagogue even existed before the Middle Ages, this theory is also discounted by most.

The third position is the one generally held today. It suggests that it was not until the Christian era that the Palestinian Jewish community closed its list of authoritative books. Jamnia, a town northwest of Jerusalem and also known as Jabneh, appears to have become the center of emerging Rabbinic Judaism after the destruction of the temple in Jerusalem. It was there that the leaders of the community made the decision about the inspired books. Just as a particular interpretation of God's presence and revelation shaped the tradition, so another particular interpretation eventually closed the list. There is no certainty about the criteria used in making this decision. It certainly was not based merely on language (though only books written in Hebrew were included) as some commentators have suggested. Knowledge of the sociopolitical and religious forces at work at that particular time in history might throw some light on this matter.

If the chosen religious traditions testify to divine revelation, then obviously the prophetic tradition, that bearer of revelation par excellence, would be included. Furthermore, only those books believed to have originated before the end of authentic prophetic activity were considered uniquely inspired. Liturgical use was probably a second criterion for determining inclusion. Books that were used in cultic or liturgical practice were included. Following such criteria a tripartite Bible soon emerged: Torah or Law (the first five books); Prophets (Former Prophets or Historical Books and Latter Prophets or the Writing Prophets); and the Writings (Psalms, Wisdom writings, the five liturgical scrolls [Song of Songs, Ruth, Lamentations, Ecclesiastes, Esther], Daniel, and the postexilic history [Ezra, Nehemiah, 1 and 2 Chronicles]). These were the sacred books of Israel that "soiled the hands." This curious phrase indicates that after handling these scrolls, the reader's hands were to be washed in a ritual acknowledgment of the holiness of the traditions and the unworthiness of the reader.

As mentioned in chapter 1, with the Hellenization of the world, the important religious traditions of Israel were translated into Greek. This Greek version was probably the one in popular use during the time of Jesus and shortly thereafter. But the Hebrew version was the one adopted by the Jewish leaders of the late first or early second century CE. Perhaps this choice was influenced by the tension that developed between the Jewish and the Christian interpretations of some of the religious traditions cherished by both religious groups. In addition to interpreting these traditions differently, Christians were adding new writings to the list of inspired traditions, writings that eventually became the New Testament.

Some scholars believe that a dispute within the Jewish community itself influenced the decision about the list of books. Some of the Jews rejected the thinking of the more apocalyptically minded Jewish sects, and, consequently, they took a stand in favor of a more conservative interpretation. The destruction of the second temple caused some to recall the time of Ezra, the time after the destruction of the first temple. At that earlier time, apocalyptic and messianic speculation had been frowned upon. Following the example of that period, the collection of books that came out of the exile at the time of Ezra became the normative version at the time of Jamnia.

The apocalyptic and messianic speculation did, however, help the Christians understand Jesus. That may be one reason why the Christians continued to use the Greek version of the ancient traditions. Whether Jesus and his disciples used the Hebrew or the Greek version is not clear. It is clear that the early Christians used the Greek version, for the Old Testament quotations found in the New Testament came from that version. This is understandable, because the vast majority of Christians of the first century were Greek-speaking converts.

In contrast to the history of the Jewish writings, the development of Christian writings and the acceptance of their canonical status are easy to trace. Witnesses to their influence can be found in the writings of the teachers of the early Christian centuries. The authority of the Christian writings rested on the fact that they preserved the authentic Jesus tradition. It was the words of Jesus that were authoritative. Paul called upon this authority in his own teaching about the Lord's final coming, "[W]e tell you this, on the word of the Lord" (1 Thess 4:15) and about the institution of the Lord's Supper, "For I received from the Lord what I also handed on to you" (1 Cor 11:23). Though oral communication was important, the need for preserving the traditions in writing soon became apparent. This was particularly true when new communities were founded far from Jerusalem and from one another. With the deaths of more and more of the eyewitnesses to Jesus, the need for authoritative written testimonies increased. Such testimonies became the building blocks of the Christian Scriptures.

By the end of the second century a new canon was taking shape, consisting of a fourfold gospel tradition and a collection of apostolic letters. The status of several of these letters was disputed as late as the fifth century. Still, early church reference to these writings and lists was the main criterion for determining their authoritative status. It was not until the second or third century that debates with the Jewish community prompted the Christians to close their own list of Jewish sacred books. Thus the church was developing a two-part canon.

By the fourth century the Western churches had accepted the decision of the early church councils and had adopted the Greek Bible. The Eastern churches, on the other hand, appear to have preferred the list of inspired books drawn up by the Jews. Since local or regional churches made such decisions, there was no consistency on the matter. It was the Council of Trent (1546) that finally decided upon the canon for the churches in union with Rome. The Roman church adopted the wider Greek canon, thus preserving an authentic early church practice. The Protestant churches retained the shorter Jewish canon, thus preserving the more ancient version.

Both Roman and Protestant traditions have the same New Testament; differences are found in the Old Testament. The canonicity of seven books is disputed. These are: Judith, Tobit, 1 and 2 Maccabees, Wisdom of Solomon, Sirach, and Baruch. These books are referred to as deuterocanonical (second-canon) by Roman Catholics, and apocryphal (set apart; inspiring but not inspired) by Protestants. Because today there is so much common biblical study among Christians of various denominations, Protestant Bibles now include these books, but under the classification of apocrypha. They are often placed as a discrete collection between the two biblical testaments.

Another group of about sixty-five Jewish writings is considered apocryphal by Roman Catholics. They include such books as Enoch, Jubilees, the Testaments of the Twelve Patriarchs, the Sibylline Oracles, the Assumption of Moses, to name but a few. Protestants classify them as pseudepigrapha (falsely ascribed) because, as was a common practice in the ancient world, these books are attributed to individuals who could not have written them.

Yet another group of writings emerged from the early Christian era. Known as Christian apocrypha, these writings include several gospels, epistles, and apocalypses. Many of them contain early Christian liturgies, prayers, dreams, and attitudes toward martyrdom. There are also pious imaginations that attempt to supply information about the life of Jesus. For various reasons, these writings were not accepted by all of the Christian communities. All of this points to the great diversity of writings that appeared in the ancient world, most of which were not included in the list of inspired writings by either Jewish or Christian communities.

Summary

Once we realize that the Bible is the word of God in human words, we realize that its message comes down to us in as great a variety of literary expressions as human beings have ever devised. When we are happy, we sing songs of joy; when we experience a setback, we complain. We praise goodness and beauty, and we condemn what is corrupt and ugly. We must remember this diversity when reading the Bible. Some of what we encounter there will be poetry and some of it prose. We must also remember that reading the Bible is a genuine cross-cultural experience. The original literary forms come from an ancient Near Eastern, unscientific, agrarian, group-oriented, patriarchal society. Understanding these literary forms is the first step in understanding the messages they are conveying.

Chapter 6

What Did They Believe?

It is difficult to separate the religious beliefs found in the Bible from the accounts of the people's experience and their social and political structures and practices. This is because the people believed that it was precisely in the midst of the events of their lives that they experienced God. They further believed that the social and political structures and practices facilitated their experience of God. Thus there was a religious dimension to those structures and practices. This was particularly true with regard to the theology of ancient Israel. Since the earliest Christian community grew out of the people of Israel, much of its theology was rooted in the religious understanding of that earlier community. Yet the distinctive faith of the early church focused on its understanding of Jesus the Christ.

"You will be my people"

The basis of the ancient Israelites' faith was the belief that they had been chosen by God from among all peoples to enjoy a special relationship with God. The people knew that they did not deserve this election. On the contrary, they regarded it as a free gift from God. In fact, they admitted that, on the international scene, they were quite insignificant: "It was not because you are the largest of all nations that the LORD set his heart on you and chose you, for you are really the smallest of all nations. It was because the LORD loved you and because of his fidelity to the oath that he swore to your fathers" (Deut 7:7-8). This is a clear declaration of

73

unmerited election. Such a statement might reflect the people's realization of their unworthiness, but it still does not explain why God chose them and not some other nation. There seems to be no other explanation than the inexplicable graciousness of God.

It should be noted that the people believed that it was God who chose Israel, not Israel who chose God. The initiative was God's, and throughout the entire Bible the stories recount that divine initiative. It was God who called Abram: "Go forth from the land of your kinsfolk and from your father's house to a land that I will show you" (Gen 12:1). It was God who inaugurated the covenant with the people: "[I]f you hearken to my voice and keep my covenant, you shall be my special possession, dearer to me than all other people, though all the earth is mine. You shall be to me a kingdom of priests, a holy nation" (Exod 19:5-6). It was God who chose David to be king: "There—anoint him, for this is he!" (1 Sam 16:12).

The same is true in the New Testament. There we read that it was God who chose Mary to be the mother of Jesus: "[T]he angel Gabriel was sent from God to a town of Galilee called Nazareth, to a virgin betrothed to a man named Joseph, of the house of David, and the virgin's name was Mary" (Luke 1:26-27). It was God who chose Paul to be the great apostle to the nations: "[T]his man is a chosen instrument of mine to carry my name before Gentiles" (Acts 9:15). Furthermore, the Christians believed that they too had been chosen by God: ". . . to us, the witnesses chosen by God in advance, who ate and drank with him after he rose from the dead" (Acts 10:41).

If it was not for some merit of their own, then why were the people of Israel chosen in the first place? It is clear that the nation as a whole and certain individuals within that nation were chosen for the sake of a particular mission. Individuals like judges, kings, prophets, and priests were selected to be spiritual leaders among the people. It was their responsibility to lead the people to fidelity to their covenant commitments. The nation as a whole was chosen to bring knowledge of the true God to the rest of the world, and this was accomplished primarily through the character of their lives.

We have already seen that the formal covenant made between God and the people through Moses required that the people live in a way appropriate to their new status as people of God. The Law set the standards for this new way of living. It directed the people to be devout and committed to God, to be honest and respectful, compassionate and forgiving toward one another. One cannot deny the fact that morality played an important role in the religious life of ancient Israel. This morality, though, should be understood as directing the people to appropriate living, rather than as restricting them from full involvement in life and happiness.

The moral dictates set out in Israel's law were meant to shape the people's lives in such a way that other nations might see their manner of living and be drawn through them to God. One passage found in the prophetic writings of both Isaiah and Micah illustrates this:

> In days to come,
> The mountain of the LORD's house
>   shall be established as the highest mountain
>   and raised above the hills.
> All nations shall stream toward it;
>   many peoples shall come and say:
> "Come, let us climb the LORD's mountain,
>   to the house of the God of Jacob,
> That he may instruct us in his ways,
>   and we may walk in his paths."
> For from Zion shall go forth instruction,
>   and the word of the LORD from Jerusalem. (Isa 2:2-3; Mic 4:1-2)

The scene depicted here is of a future time of peace and prosperity, a time when people from all nations will come to know the God of Israel because of the character of the people's lives.

The responsibilities that accompany election by God are seen in the New Testament as well. The disciples no sooner get to know a bit about Jesus than they are sent out to preach the good news to others (Matt 10:5-15; Mark 6:7-13; Luke 9:1-6). Later, in words reminiscent of God's words at Mount Sinai, the early Christians are told: "But you are 'a chosen race, a royal priesthood, a holy nation, a people of [God's] own, so that you may announce the praises' of him who called you out of darkness into his wonderful light" (1 Pet 2:9). At first they believed that only ancient Israel was chosen; later the Christian community saw itself as being the "elect of God." It gradually became clear that all people are predestined to be gathered into the community of those loved by God.

Although covenant is a political concept, in ancient Israel a rich theology developed around it. As already stated, the people believed that it was God who inaugurated the covenant, and this was done out of divine graciousness. Without denying the human obligation of adherence to the Law, other attitudes are more important to the covenant relationship, and these attitudes are associated with God rather than with the human partners. Chief among them are the three religious dispositions of loving-kindness, compassion, and fidelity.

The Hebrew word for *loving-kindness* is sometimes translated "steadfast love." It refers to the divine love that binds us to God in the covenant commitment. God is not obligated to show loving-kindness. Rather, loving-kindness is a sign or symbol of God's commitment. *Compassion*, from the word for "womb," is also translated "mercy" and denotes a deep and tender love, the kind of love a mother has for the child of her womb. This word is found in God's self-identification to Moses after the people sinned in the wilderness with the golden calf: "The LORD, the LORD, a merciful and gracious God, slow to anger and rich in kindness and fidelity" (Exod 34:6). This passage contains all three technical covenant words: mercy, kindness, and fidelity. The third word, *fidelity*, denotes "soundness" or "sure support," implying that God is totally dependable.

The loving-kindness or steadfast love, the compassion or mercy, and the fidelity that God manifests in this covenant commitment call for a response of the same sentiments from the human covenant partners. These mutual sentiments, and not simply fidelity to the Law, characterize covenant theology or spirituality. The Law directs the way covenant commitment is to be lived out; it does not define it. It shows the people how they are to be loving, merciful, and faithful.

We cannot leave our consideration of covenant theology without looking at the question of holiness. In the Bible, this characteristic is quite different from the way we understand it today. At its core is the numinous character of God, the *mysterium tremendum*, or awesome mystery. God is majestic, glorious, magnificent, all-powerful, and devoid of any hint of evil. We cannot even begin to describe God's holiness. God is set apart, different from all else. An acknowledgment of God's incomparability is behind the title "the Holy One of Israel," a title found at least twenty-five times in the writings attributed to the prophet Isaiah (Isa 1:4; 60:14). Each theophanic (manifestation of the divine) experience gave rise to religious sentiments of awe and fear, but also of fascination. We are both frightened by the total otherness of God, and inextricably drawn to it: "So Moses decided, 'I must go over to look at this remarkable sight, and see why the bush is not burned'" (Exod 3:3). But then he is told: "'Come no nearer! Remove the sandals from your feet, for the place where you stand is holy ground'" (3:5). Whatever God touches is holy or awesome, and whatever comes near to God must be holy as well.

Though God's holiness is inaccessible to human beings, they are called to a certain kind of holiness: "[Y]ou shall make and keep yourselves holy, because I am holy" (Lev 11:44). The Israelites believed that they could be holy only if they separated themselves from what was not holy. One of the most important elements of Israelite religion developed out of this desire to approach the all-holy God. Theirs was a religious system that maintained distinctions between what was holy and what was not.

The notion of holiness permeated the entire life of the Israelites. In this system of thought, holiness was understood not as virtue but as separateness. It certainly demanded a rejection of what was sinful, but it also called for separation from what is common or profane. It regulated the physical condition of the people's bodies and the food they ate, the way sacrifice was conducted, and their prescribed places in the sanctuary. Persons, places, objects, and times were holy if they were set aside for the exclusive use of God. Overseeing the distinctions between the holy or sacred and the unholy or profane was the responsibility of the priests, and the regulations that governed holiness are found in a collection of laws known as the Holiness Code (Lev 17–26). Though holiness was closely associated with ritual, it influenced all of life because the people believed that they were "a kingdom of priests, a holy nation" (Exod 19:6).

Besides regulations that governed the people, objects, times, and places involved in worship, perhaps the most important concern of the holiness tradition was the respect given to blood. This was so because of the people's reverence for life and because "the life of a living body is in its blood" (Lev 17:11, 14). Any emission of blood made one ritually unclean and prevented that person from participation in formal worship. This explains the regulations regarding menstruating women or those who had recently given birth. There was no moral judgment here. Rather, the prohibitions were a recognition of the power of blood, a power that should be separated from a comparable power present at the time of worship. Both the power of blood and ritual power were considered sacred and were to be kept away from each other, lest the combination of the two produce a force far beyond any possibility of control.

The flow of blood signified the power of life, but other bodily discharges were considered signs of disorder. This included skin lesions and running sores of any kind. Such ailments caused the person to be unclean, not because the physical condition was contagious, but because the people's sense of order required that bodily fluids belonged within the body; and any form of disorder rendered one unfit for participation in worship, or sometimes even full participation in the community that believed itself to be "a kingdom of priests, a holy nation" (Exod 19:6). This explains the segregation of those believed to have some form of leprosy and the requirement that a priest authenticate their cure (Luke 17:11-19; Lev 14:2-32). Thus holiness connotes the realm of the sacred generally, not the morally upright specifically.

An understanding of these purity laws often throws light on some aspects of the New Testament as well. This is particularly true in the story of the Good Samaritan (Luke 10:29-37). The priest and the Levite were on their way to Jerusalem, presumably to fulfill their temple responsibilities. The man who fell among robbers was left half dead at the side of the road, but these two religious functionaries were not aware of his condition. If he was dead, they would have been responsible for taking care of the body, and this would have rendered them ritually unclean and unfit for worship. Rather than take that risk, they simply passed by without looking. Understanding something of the system of ritual purity helps us to see that this story is not simply one of neighborliness. The priest and Levite chose religious performance over human compassion.

Another aspect of the holiness tradition is its system of dietary regulations. It told the people which animals could be eaten and which could not:

> any animal that has hoofs you may eat, provided it is cloven-footed and chews the cud. . . . whatever in the seas or in river waters has both fins and scales you may eat. (Lev 11:3, 9)

The reasons for such classification are lost in history. Some believe that these animals were forbidden as food because pagan nations either worshiped them or incorporated them in sacrifice, magic, or superstitious practices. Or they may have been proscribed for hygienic reasons. (Such kosher laws are observed by some religious Jews even today.)

"I will be your God"

"Hear, O Israel! The Lord is our God, the Lord alone!" (Deut 6:4). This prayer, known as the "Shema," the Hebrew form of the first word, contains what is considered the essence of the monotheistic religion of ancient Israel and Judaism to our day. Yet if monotheism is the conviction that only one God exists, then we cannot claim that the early Israelites were strict monotheists. The very earliest narratives suggest that the ancestors had devotion to household gods:

> Rachel had meanwhile appropriated her father's household idols. (Gen 31:19)

One of the first things the people did upon their entrance to the land of promise was to choose which god they would worship:

> [D]ecide today whom you will serve, the gods your fathers served beyond the River or the gods of the Amorites in whose country you are dwelling. As for me and my household, we will serve the LORD. (Josh 24:15)

They made their decision in favor of the God of Abraham, Isaac, and Jacob, obedient to the command:

> You shall not have others gods besides me. (Exod 20:3; Deut 5:7)

It is clear from passages such as these that early Israel did not observe monotheism (belief in one god), but that they practiced monolatry (worship of one god). Even in this they were not always faithful. We read that during a deadly drought, Elijah was in deadly conflict with the priests of Baal over the loyalty of the people, challenging those priests to entreat their god Baal to send rain. When their prayers went unanswered, Elijah prayed to the God of Israel, who sent rain, thus demonstrating the ineffectiveness of Baal (1 Kgs 18). The teaching of the prophet Hosea was a condemnation of Israel's participation in Canaanite fertility cults. These cults were condemned, not primarily for their sexual practices, but because the devotees looked to the Canaanite god Baal for the blessings of fertility rather than to the God of Israel.

We find evidence of such idolatry as late as the time of Jeremiah, who condemned the people for burning incense and pouring out libations to a deity known as the "queen of heaven" (Jer 44:17-19). Only gradually did the people come to see that these gods not only were powerless but were actually nonexistent. We read in the postexilic prophet Second-Isaiah:

> [The carpenter] cuts down cedars, takes a holm or an oak, and lays hold of other trees in the forest, which the Lord had planted and the rain made grow to serve man for fuel. With a part of the wood he warms himself, or makes a fire for baking bread; but with

another part he makes a god which he adores, an idol which he worships. . . . The idols have neither knowledge nor reason; their eyes are coated so that they cannot see, and their hearts so that they cannot understand. (Isa 44:14-15, 18)

The same ridicule of the gods of other nations is found in the Psalms:

Their idols are silver and gold,
the work of human hands.
They have mouths but do not speak,
eyes but do not see.
They have ears but do not hear,
noses but do not smell.
They have hands but do not feel,
feet but do not walk,
and no sound rises from their throats. (Ps 115:4-7)

The people believed that their exile in Babylon was the direct result of their failure to worship the God of Israel alone, and so from that time on they observed strict monotheism. As Israel developed its monotheistic understanding of God, it retained some of the cultic language of the neighboring polytheistic religions. This is especially true as regards some of its prayers:

Praise the God of gods;
God's love endures forever;
Praise the Lord of lords;
God's love endures forever. (Ps 136:2-3)

These titles, which suggest that God is sovereign over all other gods, can hardly be seen as examples of strict monotheism. In addition to such honorific titles, Israel also retained the concept of a heavenly court over which God rules:

The heavens praise your marvels, Lord,
your loyalty in the assembly of the holy ones. (Ps 89:6)

In other ancient religions, such a court consisted of minor deities. In Israel, it was made up of angels. The presence of such ideas is not an indication of continued polytheism. (We use similar language in our prayers today.) It is simply an example of how religious concepts and language are often retained even with slightly different meaning.

Along with the insistence on exclusive worship of God alone, the prohibition of images representing God is also found. To date, we know of no other ancient religion that forbade representing its gods in some form. Israel's prohibition is remarkable, since throughout the entire Bible God is described in anthropomorphic terms. We have already seen that God is characterized as warrior, father, mother, husband, and shepherd. Yet no depiction of these characterizations was permitted. Perhaps the human tendency of confusing the image of a god with the deity itself prompted Israel to ban all image making. Or, the prohibition may have sprung from the conviction that, though God is spoken of in anthropomorphic terms, God in fact transcends anything and everything in creation. Whatever the case may have been, the God of Israel, though intimately involved in the lives of the people, was not to be represented by any natural form.

Though there was no visual representation of God, the presence of God was often made known through some visible form:

> The Lord preceded them, in the daytime by means of a column of cloud to show them the way, and at night by means of a column of fire to give them light. (Exod 13:21)

Furthermore, Israel's monotheistic perception did not prevent it from envisioning the activity of God in various ways. The dynamic power of God was referred to as the "spirit of the LORD." This Spirit was given to various individuals at different times in Israel's history, enabling them to accomplish great feats for the entire community. Judges were endowed with the Spirit, and with the power of the Spirit they saved Israel from its enemies (Judg 3:10). This endowment was only temporary, however, lasting as long as the national threat prevailed. Kings were seized by the Spirit, providing them with the ability to govern in God's name (1 Sam 16:13). The Spirit did not make the judge or the king divine, but gave them power to act in God's stead.

Another way that divine power was seen as active in the midst of the people was through the "word of the LORD." In many traditional societies, the spoken word is thought to be a distinct reality with power to make present what it represents. Anthropologists refer to this quality as performative force. In other words, spoken language has creative power. We see this in Genesis where God simply speaks in order to bring about creation. The words are then followed by an action: "And so it happened" (Gen 1:6, 9, 11, 15, 20). This understanding of the performative power of the spoken word is behind Isaac's inability to give Esau a blessing after Jacob tricked his father into blessing him rather than his older brother. Jacob's words were already beginning to accomplish what they represented (Gen 27:33-39).

The people believed that the prophetic word functioned in this way as well. It was given to the prophet, but it was the word of God, with the power of God to effect either blessing or curse. This explains why the prophets were often persecuted or even put to death. The people were threatened by words of condemnation, and so, rather than heed the prophetic warning, they sought to silence the prophet.

Finally, divine power was shown through the mysterious figure of Wisdom, personified as a woman and found in several books of the Old Testament. Though never really identified as a divine being, Wisdom acts in ways that only God acts. This is principally evident in her presence at and activity in creation (Prov 8:30; Wis 7:22). This understanding of both the power of the word and the image of Woman Wisdom are later appropriated by the Christian community where they try to understand Jesus as the fulfillment of Jewish messianic expectations.

This Age and the Age to Come

In order to understand much of biblical thinking, one must have a good grasp of biblical eschatology. This word comes from the Greek for "talk about the end." It refers to various forms of future expectation. In a sense, the entire Bible is a story of future expectation. It begins with promises of blessing made to Abram (Gen 12:1-3) and ends with an apocalyptic vision of the fulfillment of those promises (Rev 21:1-5). More specifically, one might speak of national eschatology and personal eschatology. The former addresses the hoped-for future sociopolitical life of the people; the latter is concerned with the death and possible afterlife of the individual.

The eschatological traditions of ancient Israel began to take shape during the period of the monarchy, in particular at the time of the northern prophet Amos. He was a man from the southern kingdom of Judah who went to the northern shrine of Bethel to deliver the word of the Lord. It is in his denunciation of the northern kingdom that we find the first reference to "the day of the LORD," a concept that originally referred to a future day of punishment for the enemies of the people of God. The justice of God demanded that those who had oppressed God's people would experience God's wrath. With the denunciations of the neighboring nations by Amos, the people presumed that this dreaded day was fast approaching. However, Amos then turned toward the Israelites themselves and declared:

> Woe to those who yearn for the day of the Lord!
>   What will this day of the Lord mean for you?
>   Darkness and not light! (Amos 5:18)

Amos was troubled by the shift in land tenure policies. The poverty of some inhabitants forced them to relinquish family land holdings, allowing the wealthy to amass huge estates. This practice was diametrically opposed to the tribal federation's insistence that land be allotted along tribal or family lines. The people believed that the land really belonged to God and they only held it in trust. For this reason, it was not to be bought and sold at will. The land itself provided the security and sustenance needed to survive. During this period of history, the privileged became more and more influential, while the peasantry was disempowered and disenfranchised. It was to this socioeconomic disparity that Amos spoke.

The Israelites envisioned the day of the Lord as a time when God would intervene on their behalf. Amos turned this concept upside down, insisting that the election by God (Israel considered itself the chosen people) would not determine one's fate when this day dawned. Rather, righteous living would. If the Israelites were faithful to their covenant commitment, the day of the Lord would be a day of blessing for them; if they were not, it would be a day of doom. Subsequent prophets spoke of this day as well. Sometimes it is a day of wrath for the people of God (Isa 13:6); at other times their enemies will be afflicted (Jer 46:10). Always the judgment befalls those who have in some way been unfaithful.

After the people had endured suffering, which they interpreted as just punishment for their sins, the day of the Lord was also anticipated as a time of peace and prosperity (Isa 58:13-14). In such passages we find promises of restoration and abundance. On occasion, the prophets referred to this future with the words, "In those days . . ." (Jer 33:16; Joel 3:2). Various forms of messianic expectation developed within this eschatological tradition. One tradition looked for a descendant of David who would reestablish the royal kingdom within which the people would live in security (Isa 11:1-9). Though there is no biblical text that explicitly mentions a priestly messiah, the documents found near the Dead Sea clearly indicate that the Qumran community awaited a "Messiah of

Aaron." The book of Daniel tells of a mysterious figure, "[o]ne like a son of man" (Dan 7:13), who would establish an "everlasting dominion."

The period of history into which Jesus was born was rife with eschatological and messianic expectation. Many people were under foreign domination in their own land; their political and religious leaders were in collaboration with the Roman occupiers. There was great unrest in the land, and the people were eager for restoration of their independence. It was to such expectation that Jesus spoke when he declared, "The kingdom of God is at hand" (Mark 1:15). With these words, he declared that the day of the Lord had dawned, and the anticipated time of fulfillment had arrived.

One might wonder why Jesus was not universally accepted by the people and his words not heeded. It seems that in the beginning of his public ministry, people flocked to hear him and to benefit from his remarkable powers of healing. But as they gradually came to realize that he was not going to fulfill some of their cherished political expectations, they turned away from him in disappointment and eventually turned on him in anger. The eschatological focus of Jesus' ministry was not national fulfillment but, rather, personal and societal transformation. He called for a change in mind and heart, not in political regime. The people not only rejected him as messiah, they also rejected his version of eschatological fulfillment.

Several New Testament passages speak of "this age and the age to come" (Matt 12:32; Eph 1:21), which is a way of relating the Jewish eschatological tradition with actual chronological time. The advent of the messiah was considered the event of termination of one age and inauguration of the other. According to Jewish thinking, both of these ages would unfold within history. Christian eschatology grew out of this tradition but made some significant adjustments to it. Its claim that Jesus brought the old age to completion and opened the new age to us is in keeping with Jewish thought. Yet Jesus' death, resurrection, and ascension raised some serious questions. If we are now living in the new age, why is the world as we know it not radically changed? If this change is meant to take place when Jesus comes again, how long a time period will transpire between his resurrection-ascension and his triumphant return?

These questions have occupied the concerns of Christians. Christian theology developed an eschatological perspective that has come to be known as "already-but not yet." This means that Jesus did indeed inaugurate the new age, but it has not yet reached its full flowering. Early in his Christian career, Paul seems to have thought that he himself and his converts would live to see Christ's return. They believed that they had died with Christ and risen with him in baptism and, therefore, were preserved from physical death. This explains the Christian community's concern when some of their members began to die. Had their baptism been ineffective? Or had they been duped? Paul reassured them that those who had died would indeed rise from death (1 Thess 4:13-18). The writer of the book of Revelation declares that this period will last for a thousand years. Then Satan, who was bound during this time, will be released and will roam the earth in an attempt to gather followers to accompany him into the final battle (Rev 20:1-10). Only then will the final age dawn. Various forms of millenarianism are current today, particularly in evangelical circles; but interest in and anticipation for the end of this age captures the imagination of most people. This became quite evident as we approached the second millennium.

However long this interim period might last, in the end God will reign triumphant. The question of appropriate reward and/or punishment remains a matter of some speculation. The early Christians seem to have been more interested in the reward that faithfulness will secure, while the possibility of punishment for infidelity functioned more as a corrective than as a threat. Christians today maintain that they are living in the end time. What is not clear is whether this is merely the beginning of that end time, the middle of it, or a fast-approaching end. The New Testament writers constantly call us to be ready by living lives of integrity now.

Canonical Form

The form that the Old Testament finally took has theological significance. In the first chapters of the book of Genesis (chaps. 4–11), the stories of primeval events seem to have been arranged in order to show that as humankind became more and more technologically sophisticated, it also became more and more sinful. This may have been the early editors' way of warning the people of their time about the hidden seduction of the advances of civilization.

A more obvious example of theological editorializing is the composition of the Pentateuch itself (Torah for the Jewish people). The first five books of the Bible sketch Israel's history from the time of Abraham through the exodus account to the encampment of the people just before they crossed the Jordan River to occupy the Promised Land. This, though, is a truncated story. It does not recount the entrance into the land, which was seen as the fulfillment of the promise made to Abraham and his descendants. The people certainly had traditions about this entry by the time the first five books were considered a unit. Why did the story not include them? That would certainly have made the history more complete. As it is, the people are only on the threshold of being a people in their own land.

The decision to carve out a Pentateuch (five books) rather than a Hexateuch (six books) was probably made during the time when the people were in exile in Babylon. At that time, they were without land as their ancestors had been. In knowing that their ancestors had been unfaithful to God and were forgiven and eventually brought into the land, the later Israelites would have been encouraged to trust that God would forgive them as well and would eventually allow them also to return to the land. Thus, the very structure of the story had theological meaning.

An editorial hand can be seen in the story of Israel's life in the Promised Land (the books of Joshua, Judges, 1 and 2 Samuel, 1 and 2 Kings). A clear underlying theme can be detected in the stories of the judges. There we read that the people offended God, were punished with defeat by their enemies, cried out to God for help, and were delivered by one of their own military leaders (Judg 3:7-11). This story demonstrates the theory of retribution: sin is punished and repentance is rewarded. Though it is not as obvious as it is in the brief accounts of the judges, this theme of retribution is one of the major determining factors in the way the stories of the nation have been remembered. The entire complex of traditions is called the Deuteronomistic History because of the significance of covenant theology, with its law and subsequent rewards and punishments, found in the book of Deuteronomy.

Most scholars believe that the first two sections of religious writings, the Pentateuch or Torah and the historical books or Former Prophets had basically their present shape and content when the people went into exile. Various prophetic traditions were also preserved at that time, but it was probably during the exile that they took the shape that has come down to us today. After the exile other traditions were added to the collections; chief among them were the wisdom writings and the psalms. By the second century BCE, the Jewish community had a three-part "Bible." We read of this in the foreword to the book of Sirach or Eccleciasticus: "Many important truths have been handed down to us through the law, the prophets, and the later authors."

The order of the books in the Septuagint or Greek version is slightly different than that found in the Masoretic Text or Hebrew version. In the Hebrew version the books are ordered according to literary type. All the historical books, not merely the Deuteronomistic History, are placed after the Pentateuch. This includes Ezra, Nehemiah, and the Chronicler's History, short historical stories of Esther, Judith, and Tobit, as well as the books of the Maccabees. This is followed by books of poetry, such as Psalms and the wisdom literature. The Greek version ends with the collection of prophetic books. Some scholars believe that this kind of literary arrangement can be traced to the Hellenistic Jews who were trained in the Greek schools of rhetoric and were responsible for the Septuagint.

Finally, the way both the Jewish and the Christian collections of inspired writings end is theologically significant. The Jewish TaNaK (Torah or Law, Nebiim or Prophets, and Kethubim or Writings) ends with 2 Chronicles:

> Thus says Cyrus, king of Persia: "All the kingdoms of the earth the LORD, the God of heaven, has given to me, and he has also charged me to build him a house in Jerusalem, which is in Judah. Whoever, therefore, among you belongs to any part of his people, let him go up, and may his God be with him!" (2 Chr 36:23)

The last passage of the Jewish "Bible" is a summons to return to Jerusalem and rebuild the temple. Most likely, after the destruction of the second temple around 70 CE, the Jewish leaders arranged the books in this way for the sake of this summons. From the time of the fall of Jerusalem and the destruction of the temple at the hands of the Romans (ca. 70 CE), the Jewish people had no land of their own until 1948 when the United Nations established the state of Israel. More traditional Jews looked to this passage as a model of future redemption.

The Christian Old Testament, on the other hand, ends with the prophecy of Malachi, a name that means "my messenger." Malachi ends with a promise:

> Lo, I will send you
>   Elijah, the prophet,
> Before the day of the LORD comes,
>   the great and terrible day. (Mal 3:24)

The Gospel of Mark, considered by most scholars to be the earliest gospel, opens with the preaching of John the Baptist, perceived by New Testament writers to be:

> A voice of one crying out in the desert:
> "Prepare the way of the Lord." (Mark 1:3)

Thus the Christian arrangement of the religious traditions suggests that the New Testament theology flows out of Old Testament expectation. The arrangement of these two biblical testaments is meant to underscore the theological theme of "promise-fulfillment" as understood by the Christian community.

The placement of the book of Revelation at the end of the collection of sacred books also has theological significance. Though it belongs to the broader Johannine tradition, Revelation is not found with the gospel or letters of John. Since the content of Revelation is eschatological (end time) in nature, it brings to conclusion the entire story of salvation, which began with the promise made to Adam and Eve in the garden. It is not by accident that the popular description of the final paradise (Rev 22:1-5) resembles that of the first paradise (Gen 2:8-15). This suggests that in the end the world will be transformed and will take the shape of the original plan of God.

Although the letters of Paul were probably the earliest Christian writings, the New Testament begins with the four gospels. One might ask: "Why is it necessary to have four gospels? Wouldn't one story of the life of Jesus be enough?" That is just the point. A gospel is more than a story of the life of Jesus. It is a statement of faith in Jesus. Therefore, details about his life are interpreted and shaped so as to present a theological picture of him and his ministry, rather than merely a precise historical account. The particular theological portrait created by the respective gospel writers (Matthew, Mark, Luke, or John) is influenced by the religious needs and concerns of the communities for whom the particular gospel was originally written.

For example, an important feature of the theology of both Matthew and Mark is the reign of God and Jesus' role in inaugurating that reign. But while Matthew's Jewish-Christian community would have understood it in reference to ancient Israelite expectations, Mark's Gentile-Christian community would not. This explains some of the differences between these two gospels. Since Luke sought to present the Christian community as a reconstituted Israel, he took great pains to draw lines of continuity between these two religious groups. Finally, while the Synoptic Gospels highlight the humanness of Jesus, John concentrates on his divine sonship. From the beginning of the gospel to its end, Jesus is the glorified Word of God.

Despite their many differences, all four gospels follow basically the same literary pattern. They begin with an account of the ministry of John the Baptist and John's baptism of Jesus. This is followed by narratives that record Jesus' teaching and accounts of his healings. His final days in Jerusalem are described, as are his passion and death. The gospels end with reports of appearances of the risen Lord. Both Matthew and Luke preface their account of the public ministry with infancy narratives. Through the ages, some writers have attempted a harmonization of the four gospels in order to produce a story that reflects as closely as possible the actual events in the life of Jesus. Such attempts fail to realize the true literary character of a gospel account, and they risk missing the uniqueness of each gospel's religious message.

The order of the New Testament writings creates a kind of chronological unfolding of the Christian story. It begins with the gospel accounts of the life and ministry of Jesus. This is followed by Acts of the Apostles (believed to be a second volume written by the author of Luke's gospel), which picks up the story after the ascension of Jesus. There we read of the first years of the growth of the infant church from "Jerusalem, throughout Judea and Samaria, and to the ends of the earth" (Acts 1:8). The various letters that follow Acts provide insight into the life of the second generation of Christians. The New Testament, and indeed the entire Bible, is brought to conclusion with the book of Revelation.

"Who do you say I am?"

This is the question that Jesus asked his disciples (Matt 16:15: Mark 8:29; Luke 9:20). In all of the Synoptic Gospels, it is Peter who replies, proclaiming that Jesus is the Messiah. (In Matthew, Jesus is also identified as the Son of the living God.) Though the query is direct and the response straightforward, the writing of the entire New Testament is a further attempt to answer that question. However, the needs of the particular Christian communities for whom the respective New Testament documents were originally intended differed from place to place and so the religious message had to be shaped according to those needs. This in part explains the diversity of depictions of Jesus and the understandings of his mission that we find in the various writings.

Christ

New Testament christology, or understanding of Christ, is both complex and rich. We must remember that the first disciples of Jesus considered him the long-awaited messiah; but Israel had developed several messianic traditions (see "Covenant" in chap. 3), and so the followers of Jesus entertained various messianic expectations. Since Israel had not conceived of a suffering and dying messiah, Jesus' death threw his followers into confusion and disillusionment. Nonetheless, his appearances to them after his resurrection confirmed their faith in him, and so they began the arduous task of interpreting him in terms of earlier religious traditions, which they skillfully reinterpreted. This accounts for the diverse and at times apparently contradictory perceptions of Jesus that are found in various New Testament documents.

The issues surrounding New Testament christology can be addressed by examining some of the titles ascribed to Jesus. The first is the notion of "messiah" itself. We have already seen that the messiah was regarded by Israel as a figure who would lead the people into a future of fulfillment. Some believed that the messiah would be a king; others expected a priest; still others awaited a prophet. In the gospels Jesus is consistently depicted as rejecting the notion of kingly or royal messianism. The only place where he admits that he is a king is found in the account of his trial before Pilate, where he says: "My kingdom does not belong to this world" (John 18:36). Even with these words, he rejects any political understanding of messiah.

Nowhere in the gospels is Jesus depicted as a priestly messiah. Though Jesus broke bread and shared wine during the Last Supper, laymen also performed that ritual in ceremonial meals. Only the Letter to the Hebrews characterizes Jesus as a priest, and there the context of the sacrifice was the sanctuary in heaven and the ritual took place outside of the realm of history. Clearly, Jesus was not a Jewish priest.

A third understanding of messiah is found in the writings of the post-exilic prophet Deutero-Isaiah. There an unnamed prophet proclaims:

> The spirit of the Lord GOD is upon me,
>   because the LORD has anointed me;
> He has sent me to bring glad tidings to the lowly,
>   to heal the brokenhearted,
> To proclaim liberty to the captives
>   and release to the prisoners. (Isa 61:1)

Though in the gospels Jesus does not identify himself as a prophet, his ministry certainly does conform to this brief summary of the prophet's ministry. Perhaps it was passages such as this, which so closely resembled the public ministry of Jesus, that prompted the early Christians to identify Jesus with another Isaian prophetic figure, the servant of the Lord (Isa 42:1-4; 49:1-7; 50:4-11; 52:13–53:12). Since that servant suffered innocently at the hands of others, the gospels interpreted the passion of Jesus through the lens of this prophetic tradition.

The messianic title that is consistently ascribed to Jesus in the Synoptic tradition is "son of man." This title is an allusion to the mysterious figure found in the book of Daniel:

> One like a son of man coming,
> on the clouds of heaven;
> When he reached the Ancient One
> and was presented before him,
> He received dominion, glory, and kingship;
> nations and peoples of every language serve him.
> His dominion is an everlasting dominion
> that shall not be taken away,
> his kingship shall not be destroyed. (Dan 7:13-14)

This tradition clearly insists that the long-awaited one will not come from the ranks of a human institution like the monarchy or the priesthood, as holy and exalted as they might have been. No, the messiah would be one sent directly from God.

Though quite different in meaning, the Synoptic "son of man" has much in common with the concept of "Son of God." In the ancient world, kings were considered divine or the son of a god. Therefore, the title "son of god" was a royal title. Initially this notion that kings were somehow divine was an obstacle to Israel's acceptance of monarchy as an acceptable form of government. Eventually, however, they were able to strip the monarchy of its presumed divine character. Though on occasion they still used the title "son of God" (2 Sam 7:14; Ps 2:7), it was devoid of divine meaning. Yet when the Christians ascribed that title to Jesus, they intended the full force of its original meaning. In other words, just as ancient Israel had emptied the title of divine significance, the followers of Jesus restored its original sense. At the time of Jesus, the monarchy had lost its religious significance and was merely a puppet political institution. Thus the title was probably understood as a reference to God and not to the king. This understanding was reinforced by the fact that their Roman occupiers used the identical title in reference to Caesar. This would explain the Jews' passionate resistance to any application of the title to Jesus. To consider Jesus divine would have been seen as a violation of monotheistic faith.

We find the beginnings of trinitarian faith as early as the writings of Paul. There Jesus is clearly identified as the Son of God (1 Cor 1:9). Once Jesus was understood in this way, his divine nature became the lens through which later authors, the gospel writers among them, described him. It is important to remember that all of the New Testament was written after Jesus' resurrection; and it was written by people who believed that Jesus had indeed been raised from the dead, and so he is often depicted as possessing abilities that would flow from that exalted state. In other words, all New Testament writings are statements of faith, not of history. This does not mean that they are not true. It means, rather, that they have religious rather than merely historical significance.

Christian theology speaks of both a "low christology" and a "high christology." The former focuses on Jesus the man who "has similarly been tested in every way, yet without sin" (Heb 4:15). This is the point of view that we find in the Synoptic Gospels, where Jesus' life, ministry, and death are recounted. The latter perspective portrays a more exalted Jesus, one who enjoys a unique union with God and extraordinary powers that flow from such a union. This is the Jesus of the resurrection, the Jesus that Paul knew and about whom he wrote. It should be clear from this brief overview that there is no simple answer to the question: "Who do you say I am?"

Salvation/redemption

Salvation is one of the most fundamental concepts of the Bible. It was out of God's saving act of deliverance from Egypt that the nation of Israel was born; and Christian faith is rooted in the salvation realized through Christ. In ancient Israel, the experience of past deliverance raised the hope of salvation in the future. This hope was intimately linked with other messianic hopes. Initially this hope was political rather than spiritual. Even in those passages that envision a restored nation, however, there is a presumption that this new Israel would really be a new creation, purified of sin. It is in New Testament theology that we find a slightly different understanding of salvation. There it is concerned with the inner life or being of the person.

Two words that Paul uses quite frequently are "salvation" and "redemption." Though these words are frequently used interchangeably, they have distinctly different meanings. The word "salvation" presumes that there is a danger from which one cannot save oneself. As ancient

Israel used the term, the danger might have been political, as in the case of oppression in Egypt or exile in Babylon. Or it might have been personal misfortune, as experienced by Job. Whether political and social or personal and individual, the need for salvation does not always imply guilt on the part of the one suffering. Hence, while misfortune was then and even today continues to be interpreted as punishment for sinfulness, relevant passages in the Old Testament, particularly from the prophets and from Job, show that many suffering people are innocent of transgression. Jesus, Stephen, and Paul are New Testament examples of innocent people who suffer terribly.

As important as the concept of salvation was to the early Christians, the word itself seldom appears in their writings. In the gospels, when Jesus speaks of salvation it is usually associated with the establishment of the reign of God. When he forgives the woman who bathed his feet in her tears, he reassures her: "Your faith has saved you; go in peace" (Luke 7:50); or speaking to Zacchaeus he says: "Today salvation has come to this house" (19:9). It is really Paul who develops a theology of salvation.

According to Paul, salvation occurs only in and through Christ. This conviction is not merely the fruit of Paul's own extraordinary conversion. It flows from his understanding of Jesus' very name, which comes from *yeshu'ah*, the Hebrew word for salvation. The angel who reassured Joseph to take Mary as his wife foretold Jesus' name and destiny in life: "She will bear a son and you are to name him Jesus, because he will save his people from their sins" (Matt 1:21). This statement provides the ultimate focus for an understanding of salvation. Since it basically means deliverance from some evil, and since sin is the ultimate evil, the New Testament uses "salvation" mainly in the sense of liberation of the human race or of an individual from sin and its consequences.

The notion of sin immediately introduces the concepts of divine forgiveness and grace. Sin is more than the violation of some directive. It is better defined as opposition to God's gracious purposes for creation. While some of the biblical terms for sin do indeed signify deliberate rejection and defiance, the most common words in both Hebrew and Greek imply "missing the mark" or falling short of God's expectations. The mythological story in the book of Genesis blames sin on a tempting serpent. Yet there are enough examples of sin throughout the entire Bible to point the finger of blame at human pride and selfishness.

Despite human failure, God's graciousness far exceeds the power of sin. Multiple examples of God's forgiveness appear in the Old Testament. Again and again, Israel sinned; again and again, God forgave the people.

The book of Hosea, with its story of betrayed love and ultimate forgiveness, is a prime example of human infidelity and divine graciousness. The definitive instance of God's love and mercy, though, is found in the New Testament. It is there that we read: "But God proves his love for us in that while we were still sinners Christ died for us" (Rom 5:8). This is a classic example of divine grace.

The word "grace" means favor, God's favor toward us. The Old Testament provides many examples of divine favor: the election of Israel as the special people of God, and God's deliverance of the people from bondage in Egypt and from exile in Babylon. "Grace" really comes from the Greek, and its meaning holds a prominent place in New Testament theology. There it is used in two different but closely related ways. First, it refers to divine favor just as it is found in the Old Testament. Though it does not contain the word "grace," one of the most familiar passages describing God's graciousness, or favor, is found in John's gospel:

> For God so loved the world that he gave his only Son, so that everyone who believes in him might not perish but might have eternal life. (John 3:16)

Paul claims that, like the Jews before them, Christians enjoy election by God because of God's graciousness, not because of some merit of their own. Thus Paul insists:

> So also at the present time there is a remnant, chosen by grace. But if by grace, it is no longer because of works; otherwise grace would no longer be grace. (Rom 11:5-6)

Grace also designates the divine power given to believers enabling them to live lives of righteousness after the model of Jesus:

> Now Stephen, filled with grace and power, was working great wonders and signs among the people. (Acts 6:8)

As mentioned above, salvation and redemption are frequently used interchangeably. While they both denote gracious acts, the terms are quite different. Redemption originally referred to an ancient family practice of debt payment. If someone was unable to meet an obligation, that person was often cast into prison until the debt was paid. In such cases, a family member was expected to step in and "redeem" the debtor. Thus redemption meant paying the debt of another; and the redeemer was the one who paid. This ancient Israelite custom became a metaphor for the salvation that Jesus won for us. In the letter to the Ephesians we read that his blood was the price paid for the debt that we owed:

> In him we have redemption by his blood, the forgiveness of transgressions, in accord with the riches of his grace. (Eph 1:7)

Redemption is like salvation in that it is salvific. However, unlike salvation, the concept of redemption includes a definite dimension of debt payment. This concept, used as a metaphor to describe God's graciousness to sinful human beings, allows Paul to develop the notion of recompense for sin. In other words, human sinfulness has put us in God's debt. Since we all sin, we are all in debt to God. Because of our creatureliness, we cannot hope to make adequate amends, and so we always stand in judgment before God; but through the graciousness of God our debt has been paid by Christ.

Another ancient Israelite custom is employed to describe payment of this debt. It is the traditional practice of blood sacrifice (see "Worship and Prayer" in chap. 3). The Pauline interpretation of the death of Jesus contains elements of two major Israelite sacrifices, though it fits neither of them perfectly. The first sacrifice is the holocaust, which was usually offered in order to expiate, or make atonement for, sin:

> [Sinners] are justified freely by [God's] grace through the redemption in Christ Jesus, whom God set forth as an expiation, through faith, by his blood. (Rom 3:24)

While Jesus' sacrifice is understood as an act of atonement, it did not include total destruction by fire, as the holocaust did. The second sacrifice is the peace offering:

> For in [Christ] all the fullness was pleased to dwell,
>   and through him to reconcile all things for [God]
> making peace by the blood of his cross. (Col 1:19-20)

The peace offering was also a bloody sacrifice, but it included a communion meal participated in by those who offered the sacrifice. Since this sacrifice had first been offered to God, the meal signified communion with God.

The early Christian teaching about salvation and redemption by Christ is both rich and complex. This is because various ancient practices and religious metaphors very different from each other were later reinterpreted by the New Testament authors. The reinterpretation of these practices and metaphors allowed creative new insights to emerge. The teaching that resulted may be confusing and may even appear to be contradictory if we try to make details of one theme fit neatly with details of another. The mystery of God's graciousness to us through Christ is too profound to be captured in one theological image.

Church

The gospels are filled with references to the reign of God. The word "church," though, is found in only two passages, both of which are in Matthew's gospel. The most familiar passage marks the establishment of the church:

> . . . you are Peter, and upon this rock I will build my church, and the gates of the netherworld shall not prevail against it. I will give you the keys to the kingdom of heaven. Whatever you bind on earth shall be bound in heaven; and whatever you loose on earth shall be loosed in heaven. (Matt 16:18-19)

There is a play on the name Peter and rock. Both words are translations of the Aramaic word *kêpā'*. The gospels go to great lengths in showing that Peter, the foundation of the church, is a weak human being. This may well have been a way of keeping the church humble and dependent on the graciousness of God for its survival and growth. The keys signify authority, an indication that decisions made by the church have heavenly authorization. The second passage containing the word "church" (18:17) demonstrates how that authority is to be exercised, not merely by the designated leader but by the entire assembly of disciples. It describes how an erring member of the church is to be treated.

The Greek word for church is *ekklēsía*, which means "assembly of people." In the Septuagint (the Greek version of the Bible), *ekklēsía* is used interchangeably with *synagogē*, another Greek word for assembly. Over the years, *synagogē* came to designate the Jewish assembly, while *ekklēsía* referred to the Christian gathering. Since the Christian gathering grew out of the Jewish assembly, in the beginning there was probably little difference between the outer appearances of their respective services. There would have been reading of the Scriptures and interpretation of its meaning, along with prayers. On special occasions there might be a ceremonial meal. Here the religious differences would have been obvious. The Jewish memorial meal commemorated that community's deliverance from Egyptian bondage, while the Christians' ceremony commemorated the death and resurrection of Jesus. As the two groups gradually distinguished themselves from each other, their respective manners of assembly also became distinct.

The first passage mentioned above (Matt 16:18-19) provides us with an insight into the nature of the church. In this passage the church is not identified as the reign of God, but it opens the doors to that reign so that people can enter it. In other words, the church mediates God's salvific graciousness to those who seek to be part of God's reign. The passage does not promise to preserve believers from the onslaughts of evil, but to protect them from ultimate defeat. Roman Catholics believe that this passage supports their belief that the successor of Peter, the reigning pope, has jurisdiction over the entire Christian community. Protestants may recognize the importance of that successor, but they question the extent of his jurisdiction. However this issue is understood, all Christians recognize the significance of the passage in grasping the meaning of church.

New Testament scholars consider the very early church as one of the many movements within Judaism of the time. They refer to it as the "Jesus movement." It is this period of the church that is described in the first part of the Acts of the Apostles (chaps. 1–12):

> They devoted themselves to the teaching of the apostles and to the communal life, to the breaking of the bread and to the prayers. . . . All who believed were together and had all things in common. . . . Every day they devoted themselves to meeting together in the temple area and to breaking bread in their homes. (Acts 2:42, 44, 46)

In this initial stage, the church is frequently referred to as the *koinōnia*, or community, because the members believed that they had so much in common. The period is also called the Apostolic Age, because the leaders in the church were the original apostles.

It is in the writings of Paul that we find a more structured development within the various groups of believers. It is Paul who used the word "church" to designate the gathering of those who believe in Jesus. Like other voluntary associations of that time, these believers met in each others' homes. Thus began what came to be known today as "house churches." In his letters, Paul often sent greetings to the members of such house churches:

> Greet Prisca and Aquila . . . greet also the church at their house.
> (Rom 16:3, 5)

> Give greetings to the brothers in Laodicea and to Nympha and to
> the church in her house. (Col 4:15)

It was in houses such as these that the "Lord's Supper" was celebrated.

Though Paul usually began his preaching in the synagogues of the Jews, he eventually turned his attention to the Gentile world. This move precipitated the first real crisis that faced the infant church. Since the early Christians believed that "salvation is from the Jews" (John 4:22), they held that it was necessary for Gentile converts to observe Jewish religious customs in order to belong to the church. Some of the Jewish Christians insisted: "Unless you are circumcised according to the Mosaic practice, you cannot be saved" (Acts 15:1). On this matter "there arose no little dissension and debate by Paul and Barnabas" (15:2). This disagreement was settled by a compromise issued by the leaders of the Jerusalem community:

> It is the decision of the holy Spirit and of us not to place on you
> any burden beyond these necessities, namely, to abstain from meat
> sacrificed to idols, from blood, from meats of strangled animals, and
> from unlawful marriage. (Acts 15:28-29)

With the decision not to require circumcision, the church had taken a significant turn away from its Jewish roots.

During the post–Apostolic Age (after 65 CE) the church took on an increasingly definite structure. This can be clearly seen in the post–Pauline Letters. It is there that we find references to bishops, also called overseers, who have the responsibility of governing the church (1 Tim 3:1; Titus 1:7-9). As significant as the evolving church structure might have been and continues to be, what is most important is the actual community of believers. This community was primarily characterized by Paul as "the body of Christ."

The image of the "body of Christ" is one of the most profound metaphors for the church, capturing several of its important features. First, it acknowledges that the diversity within the community of believers is necessary and enriching rather than threatening and divisive:

> But as it is, there are many parts, yet one body. The eye cannot say
> to the hand, "I do not need you," nor again the head to the feet, "I
> do not need you." (1 Cor 12:20-21)

Second, it characterizes the church as a living, growing assembly of members:

> For as in one body we have many parts, and all the parts do not have the same function, so we, though many, are one body in Christ and individually parts of one another. (Rom 12:4-5)

Third, and perhaps most important, it identifies this group as a vital manifestation of Christ present in the world today:

> [W]e should grow in every way into him who is the head, Christ, from whom the whole body, joined and held together by every supporting ligament, with the proper functioning of each part, brings about the body's growth and builds itself up in love. (Eph 4:15-16)

This image of church as the "body of Christ" portrays what the church in fact is, while at the same time it challenges the members to become ever truer to their exalted identity. Once again we see the "already-but not yet" character of Christian life. This challenge put forward by the notion of "body of Christ" explains Paul's constant insistence on ethical behavior:

> Put on then, as God's chosen ones, holy and beloved, heartfelt compassion, kindness, humility, gentleness, and patience, bearing with one another and forgiving one another, if one has a grievance against another; as the Lord has forgiven you, so must you also do. And over all these put on love, that is, the bond of perfection. (Col 3:12-14)

If the church is the "body of Christ," then its members must model their behavior after the behavior of Christ.

The challenge of growing deeper and deeper into the mystery of being Christ in the world presents itself in the day-to-day experiences of life in an extraordinary way of transformation. This transformation is accomplished principally through sharing the eucharistic meal:

> Because the loaf of bread is one, we, though many, are one body, for we all partake of the one loaf. (1 Cor 10:17)

When we eat natural bread, we make it part of ourselves. When we eat the bread that is the eucharistic body of Christ, we, with everyone else who feeds on that bread, mysteriously become part of that "Body of Christ."

The resolution of the first major conflict within the church taught the early Christians, and us, that circumcision was not the way into the church. Jesus declared that it was faith that brought people into the reign of God (Matt 9:2; Mark 5:34; Luke 18:42), and Paul insisted that faith alone was necessary for salvation: "[A] person is justified by faith apart from works of the law" (Rom 3:28). At the same time, there were rituals that marked one's entrance into the church. They included baptism and anointing with the Spirit.

All of the gospels recount Jesus' own baptism in the Jordan River by John the Baptist. This baptism reflects a common Jewish cultic rite of purification performed by religious Jews of the time. The baptism that John performed, though, was not cultic in orientation, but penitential, "for the forgiveness of sins" (Mark 1:4; Luke 3:3). This orientation explains why John initially objected to Jesus' desire to be baptized. Only when Jesus insisted, did John perform the ritual (Matt 3:13-15). The baptism practiced by the church was different from both the Jewish purification rite and John's penitential devotion. It was considered the believer's first ritual participation in the death and resurrection of Jesus:

> [A]re you unaware that we who were baptized into Christ Jesus were baptized into his death? We were indeed buried with him through baptism into death, so that, just as Christ was raised from the dead by the glory of the Father, we too might live in newness of life. (Rom 6:3-4)

This ritual initiation into the community of believers followed the injunction Jesus gave his disciples just before he ascended into heaven:

> Go, therefore, and make disciples of all nations, baptizing them in the name of the Father, and of the Son, and of the holy Spirit. (Matt 28:19)

Though we today are quite familiar with this particular baptismal formula, there seem to have been several such formulae in use in the early church. Peter uses a different formula in his instruction to those Jews who heard his bold speech on the feast of Pentecost:

> Repent and be baptized, every one of you, in the name of Jesus Christ for the forgiveness of your sins; and you will receive the gift of the holy Spirit. (Acts 2:38)

Sometimes the Holy Spirit descends upon the person before baptism (Acts 10:44), and sometimes after the rite is performed (8:15-17; 19:5-6). This apparent discrepancy and the various baptismal formulae show that the early church had not yet formalized its sacramental practice or understanding.

According to Paul, the Spirit plays an active role in the baptism of believers:

> [Y]ou have had yourselves washed, you were sanctified, you were justified in the name of the Lord Jesus Christ and in the Spirit of our God. (1 Cor 6:11)

If believers were made children of God at the time of their baptism, it was through the power of the Spirit that this was accomplished:

> For those who are led by the Spirit of God are children of God. (Rom 8:14)

It was through this same power that the church was established:

> For in one Spirit we were all baptized into one body, whether Jews of Greeks, slaves or free persons, and we were all given to drink of one Spirit. (1 Cor 12:13)

The New Testament writers' teaching on the role of the Spirit in the initiation of members into the church touches on several aspects of early Christian theology. The Spirit was believed to be the dynamic underpinning of the church itself, the mystical bond that joins members to each other, the divine force operative in sacramental practice. Here we see the beginnings of a definite trinitarian theology.

Spirit

The Spirit is the dynamic, animating presence of God in the world. In the Old Testament, the Spirit is referred to as the Spirit of God or the Spirit of the Lord, and this Spirit is found in several extraordinary circumstances. Ancient Israel's understanding of God did not include a trinitarian dimension, and so this Spirit was considered merely a manifestation of the all-powerful God.

The Spirit of the Lord plays a significant role at the time of the judges (ca. 1200–1000 BCE). They were the military leaders who passed judgment on the enemies of Israel on the battlefields. Again and again we read that "the spirit of the LORD came upon him" (Judg 3:10; cf. 6:34; 11:29; 13:25; 14:6, 19; 15:14). The Spirit provided extraordinary ability to the ones upon whom the Spirit descended, enabling them to perform feats that far exceeded their normal behavior. Gideon is a prime example of this. When the angel of the Lord came to him with the message that he had been chosen to deliver the Israelites from the power of the Midianites, Gideon responded: "I am the most insignificant in my father's house" (Judg 6:15). Gideon tried ruse after ruse to dissuade the angel, but he finally conceded to God's wishes. Then "the spirit of the LORD enveloped Gideon; he blew the horn that summoned Abiezer to follow him" (6:34).

The Spirit was not a permanent possession of the judges. They did not determine when or where the power given through the Spirit was to be exercised. That was God's decision. When the people were threatened with destruction at the hands of a more powerful nation, God intervened. Choosing an individual through whom to work, God saved the people from their plight. When the threat no longer existed, the Spirit withdrew. It is clear that the power of the Spirit was not a personal possession of the individual. Rather, the one with that power was thought to be possessed by the Spirit, and only for the sake of the community.

The Spirit of God also possessed the first two kings of Israel. Along with a later anointing, this experience of the Spirit was the sign of God's choice of them as rulers of the people:

> [A] band of prophets met [Saul], and the spirit of God rushed upon him. (1 Sam 10:10)

> Then Samuel, with the horn of oil in hand, anointed him in the midst of his brothers; and from that day on, the spirit of the LORD rushed upon David. (1 Sam 16:13)

The story of Saul is one of initial devotion and success, but eventual failure and despair. Since what the Bible says about him probably comes from followers of David, we presume that these stories were told with a definite Davidic bias. They portray Saul more as a successful warrior than as an able administrator. We read that at the end of his life "The spirit of the LORD had departed from Saul, and he was tormented by an evil spirit sent by the LORD" (1 Sam 16:14). The reign of David is described quite differently. He had been endowed with the Spirit at the time of his anointing, and there is no indication that the Spirit of the Lord ever left him. In fact, the last testament of David makes a bold claim:

These are the last words of David:
> "The utterance of David, son of Jesse;
>> the utterance of the man God raised up,
> Anointed of the God of Jacob,
>> favorite of the Mighty one of Israel.
> The spirit of the LORD spoke through me;
>> his word was on my tongue." (2 Sam 23:1-2)

In this passage, not only does David claim to have ruled through the power of the Spirit, but he claims that his rulings enjoyed divine legitimation. David's words were not considered prophetic, for he had been chosen to rule the people, not to deliver God's word to them, as was the responsibility of the prophets.

When the prophets recount their experience of God, they report that it was the word of the Lord that came to them, not the Spirit of the Lord (Isa 38:4; Jer 1:2; Ezek 1:3; Hos 1:1; Joel 1:1; Jonah 1:1; Mic 1:1; Hag 1:1; Zech 1:1; Mal 1:1). Isaiah, though, announces that the messianic figure of the future will be filled with the Spirit of the Lord:

> The spirit of the LORD shall rest upon him. (Isa 11:2)

> Here is my servant whom I uphold,
>> my chosen one with whom I am pleased,
> Upon whom I have put my spirit. (Isa 42:1)

> The spirit of the Lord GOD is upon me,
>> because the LORD has anointed me. (Isa 61:1)

The prophet Joel makes an even bolder claim when he says:

> Then afterward I will pour out
>> my spirit upon all mankind.
> Your sons and daughters shall prophesy,
>> your old men shall dream dreams,
>> your young men shall see visions;
> Even upon the servants and the handmaids,
>> in those days, I will pour out my spirit. (Joel 3:1-2)

According to this passage, in the eschatological time of fulfillment, the Spirit will be given not only to select individuals but to all humankind. Furthermore, there will be no distinctions according to gender ("sons and daughters"), or age ("old men . . . young men"), or social class ("servants and handmaids").

This rich tradition of the Spirit of the Lord lent itself to reinterpretation and development by New Testament writers. According to the writers of the infancy narratives, Jesus was conceived by the Holy Spirit (Matt 1:18-20; Luke 1:35). All of the gospel writers report that the Spirit descended upon Jesus at the time of his baptism by John in the Jordan River (Matt 3:16; Mark 1:10; Luke 3:22; John 1:33). Following this, though, there is little mention of the Spirit until the end of Jesus' life, when he promised to send the Spirit to continue the work that he had begun (John 14:26; 15:26; 16:13-14).

There are two major dimensions to the New Testament teaching about the Spirit. The first is trinitarian, addressing the relationship between Jesus and the Spirit of God. The second focuses on the role of the Spirit in the life of the believers. An explanation of the first dimension is found in John's account of Jesus' last discourse delivered the night before he died (John 14–16). The role played by the Spirit in the church is a favorite theme of Paul and is found in several of his letters.

In his final discourse, Jesus spoke about returning to God whom he called "Father." Responding to Philip's request to be shown this Father, Jesus indicated the intimate relationship between this Father and himself with the words: "Do you not believe that I am in the Father and the Father is in me?" (John 14:10). In an attempt to comfort his disciples who were disturbed when they heard that he would be leaving them, he promised that the Father would send the Spirit to them: "And I will ask the Father, and he will give you another Advocate [Paraclete] to be with you always, the Spirit of truth, which the world cannot accept, because it neither sees nor knows it" (14:16-17).

The word *paraklētos*, which this gospel alone employs, comes from the Greek meaning "call in to help." The word has a legal connotation, suggesting legal assistance in court. This connotation throws light on why this Advocate is also called the Spirit of truth. Jesus has just promised that his followers will be able to do greater works than he did (14:12). These very works will put them at odds with the "world" that is blind to the truth. They will need an Advocate to counsel them, a Comforter to strengthen them.

Jesus has already indicated that he and the Father are one. He continues his explanation of his relationship with the Father and with the Spirit by stating that the Advocate, the Holy Spirit, will be sent by the Father in Jesus' own name (John 14:26). So the Spirit is sent by the Father in the name of the Son. The union of the three is further stated: "When the Advocate comes whom I will send you from the Father, the Spirit of truth that proceeds from the Father, he will testify to me" (15:26). The apparent discrepancy in these passages led to a serious controversy in the first centuries of the church. Some, quoting John 14:16 and 26, claimed that the Spirit proceeded only from the Father. Others insisted that the Spirit proceeded from the Son as well, arguing from John 15:26. A later council of the church made the decision in favor of double procession. Today in their liturgy, Roman Catholics profess the Nicene-Constantinopolitan creed, which includes:

> We believe in the Holy Spirit,
> the Lord, the giver of life,
> who proceeds from the Father and the Son.

In his teaching of the early Christian communities, Paul developed the ancient Israelite concept of the Spirit of the Lord taking possession of believers. He went on to describe how the gift of the Spirit transformed their lives. He did recognize that believers were endowed with "gifts of the Spirit" meant to enrich the entire community: "There are different kinds of spiritual gifts but the same Spirit" (1 Cor 12:4). These gifts include wisdom, knowledge, faith, healing, mighty deeds, prophecy discernment of spirits, tongues, and interpretation of tongues (12:8-10). Though Paul did place high values on the gifts of the Spirit bestowed on the Christians, he was more interested in the effects of the Spirit in the world.

First, Paul credited the growth of the church to the action of the Spirit:

> The church throughout all Judea, Galilee, and Samaria was at peace. It was being built up and walked in the fear of the Lord, and with the consolation of the holy Spirit it grew in numbers. (Acts 9:31)

Furthermore, it was the Spirit who directed the apostles out of the confines of the Jewish world into the Gentile world:

> [T]he holy Spirit said, "Set apart for me Barnabas and Saul for the work to which I have called them." (Acts 13:2)

It is in the letters that Paul wrote to his Gentile converts that we find Paul's most explicit teaching about the transformation that the Spirit will accomplish in the lives of believers. He draws lines of distinction between living a life "in the flesh" and living "in the spirit"

(Rom 8:1-13). By "flesh" he means human weakness, and so a life "in the flesh" is a life of:

> . . . immorality, impurity, licentiousness, idolatry, sorcery, hatreds, rivalry, jealousy, outbursts of fury, acts of selfishness, dissensions, factions, occasions of envy, drinking bouts, orgies, and the like. (Gal 5:19-21)

On the other hand, a life "in the spirit" is one of:

> . . . love, joy, peace, patience, kindness, generosity, faithfulness, gentleness, self-control. (Gal 5:22-23)

Christians are called to live "in the Spirit" because they are temples of God and the Spirit of God lives in them (1 Cor 3:16; 6:19).

Most people are familiar with the famous passage from 1 Corinthians in which Paul sings praises to love (13:1-13). There is a perhaps less-known passage in another letter that reminds us of the origin of such love:

> [T]he love of God has been poured out into our hearts through the holy Spirit that has been given to us. (Rom 5:5)

This love has been bestowed on us so that we might love others with the love of God.

Finally, there is an eschatological character to Paul's understanding of the Spirit. The Spirit is the first installment of the future inheritance promised to us (2 Cor 1:22; Eph 1:14). Because of the Spirit who dwells within us, we can rest assured that our redemption is secured. We have been made heirs with Christ (Rom 8:17). The Spirit is the ultimate gift of God's presence within us in this life and the pledge of the fullness of life in the age to come. A passage from the letter to Titus captures many facets of the mystery of our salvation:

> But when the kindness and generous love
>   of God our savior appeared,
> not because of any righteous deeds we had done
>   but because of his mercy,
> he saved us through the bath of rebirth
>   and renewal by the holy Spirit,
> whom he richly poured out on us
>   through Jesus Christ our savior,

so that we might be justified by his grace
and become heirs in hope of eternal life. (Titus 3:4-7).

Summary

Covenant is the core concept of biblical faith. This is a relationship of binding commitment of both parties. Throughout both testaments of the Bible, we find that God is always the one who initiates this relationship. God promises to be faithful to the responsibilities of the covenant and requires that we do the same. The blessings of our life are evidence of God's fidelity. All of the religious practices and customs that have grown up over the ages are examples of our attempt to be faithful. Despite God's constant fidelity toward us, we often fail to stand fast on our part. Yet biblical faith is always future-orientated. We look forward to a time when we will no longer fail, a time when, because of the death and resurrection of Jesus, our covenant relationship with God will no longer be threatened, and we will be joined in everlasting faithfulness.

Part III

What Does It Mean?

Perhaps the most challenging aspect of biblical study today is the area called hermeneutics. The word is derived from the Greek for "interpret" or "explain." Yet hermeneutics is more than simple explanation. It presumes a cultural difference between the writer and the reader that prevents the message from being immediately grasped by the reader. Both the word and the meaning of hermeneutics are related to the Greek god Hermes who was the interpreter of the messages of the gods. There is a tradition in Greek mythology that this god often played tricks on those to whom he was supposed to deliver messages. In fact, he sometimes changed the message, thus influencing its meaning. This deception hints at the ever present need for careful interpretation of any message.

Biblical hermeneutics consists of two important steps: exegesis, which includes analysis; and interpretation itself. The exegesis uncovers the many facets of the content of the passage; the analysis seeks to discover the meaning of the passage. Some would say that the real meaning is the original meaning intended by the author. In other words: "What *did* it mean?" Interpretation presumes that this first step has been accomplished; it then moves beyond this original meaning in order to make it relevant in a new context. This move is called recontextualization (moving it from one context to another). This approach is concerned with a second question: "What *does* it mean today?"

The distinction between what it meant in the past and what it might mean today raises an important question: is it possible that the same message can be heard in different ways in different contexts? Hermeneutics would answer this question positively. It argues that it might well have the same basic meaning in both situations, but it can function in different ways in each. It is at this point that hermeneutics makes a subtle but extremely important distinction between understanding the meaning and appropriating that meaning into one's life. An example might demonstrate this.

Two congregations hear the same gospel promise that "the poor shall inherit the earth" (a paraphrase of one of the Beatitudes [Matt 5:5]). One group lives in a depressed section of town; the other is located in a wealthy suburb. Both groups hear the message and know what it means. Yet their different social contexts influence them to understand that message in very different ways. The poor might either find hope in the promise of a better life, or cynically dismiss the promise, believing that nothing is going to change. The wealthy might be challenged by the message, either fearing that they will lose what they consider their own, or inspired to share with those less fortunate. It is easy to see that the disposition of the hearer influences how the message is understood or appropriated.

Within the recent past, scholars have come to realize that there are three basic approaches to interpreting a biblical passage. An approach can be author-centered, text-centered, or reader-centered. Each approach calls for a distinctive method of interpretation. An author-centered approach employs various historical-critical methods; a text-centered approach usually prefers some form of literary criticism; a reader-centered approach takes into consideration the sociocultural reality of the readers. While it is easy to distinguish these three approaches on paper, biblical scholars generally employ aspects of each approach when interpreting a biblical passage.

It is clear that context plays an important role in the interpretation of a passage. But which context? The historical context of the author? The literary context within which the passage is found? Or the context of the contemporary reader? Actually, as different as these contexts may be, each one is important because it determines the focus of one of the three interpretive approaches mentioned above. The author-centered approach attempts to reconstruct the context or historical world of the author or the original community. The text-centered approach is concerned with the context or world that is fashioned within the passage itself. The reader-centered approach focuses on the context or actual social location of the reader. Each approach yields insights into the many-layered message of the passage. Together they provide a treasure trove of religious meaning.

Finally, though a critical examination and interpretation of a passage appears to be complicated, many of the steps of the process are actually operative in the ordinary act of reading. Hermeneutical theories simply attempt to make explicit the subtle and implicit workings of the human mind.

Chapter 7

How Did They Do It?

The fact that the Bible has meant different things to different people is not new. We are all acquainted with biblical controversies in which opposing sides claim that their interpretation, and only theirs, is the true meaning of the passage and all others are false. An overview of the history of the Bible will show that across the centuries believers have, at various times, used different methods of interpretation; and different methods yield different understandings. The Bible itself contains examples of this variety.

Rewriting

The prophet Isaiah described Israel's return from Babylonian exile as a journey through the wilderness:

> A voice cries out:
> In the desert prepare the way of the LORD!
> Make straight in the wasteland a highway for our God! (Isa 40:3)

At a later time and in different circumstances, the gospel writers employed this same passage in their description of John the Baptist:

> A voice of one crying out in the desert,
> "Prepare the way of the Lord,
> make straight his paths." (Matt 3:3; cf. Mark 1:3; Luke 3:4;
> John 1:23)

By recontextualizing this passage, the evangelists gave it a new and significantly different meaning. In the Isaian passage, the focus is the "way of the LORD" in the wilderness. The gospels shift the focus slightly by having the "voice of one crying out" as its focus. This method of rewriting was a common Jewish interpretive approach, evident in both the Old and the New Testaments. In fact, much of the New Testament developed out of the method of rewriting. Luke does this very thing when, in his account of Jesus' preaching to and rejection by the people of Nazareth (Luke 4:16-30), he weaves together two passages from the writings of the prophet Isaiah (Luke 4:18-19; see Isa 61:1-2; 58:6).

Prefigurement/Typology

The Bible of the earliest Christians was the same as that of the Jewish community and so was their method of interpretation; but when the Christians began to preach Jesus as the fulfillment of their religious expectations, their interpretations took on a distinctively different character. The primary focus of their understanding was no longer Jewish law and tradition, but Jesus crucified and risen. Typology, or prefigurement, and allegory became popular methods of interpretation for accomplishing this. The use of these techniques is also found in the biblical writings themselves. For example, salvation from the waters of the flood in the days of Noah was seen as a prefigurement of salvation through the waters of baptism (1 Pet 3:21).

In his letter to the Romans, Paul uses typology. He argues that one person can stand for and act in the name of an entire group. In doing so, he maintains that Adam, whose disobedience made everyone a sinner, is a type of Christ, whose obedience made everyone righteous (Rom 5:14-19). Paul also made an allegorical comparison between Abraham's wives, Sarah and Hagar, and the Christian and Jewish communities: "Now this is an allegory. These women represent two covenants" (Gal 4:24).

Allegory

Allegory soon became one of the most prominent techniques of Christian interpretation. At various points in history, the circumstances facing the early church influenced its development and use. For instance, the church employed allegory to support its religious claims when it was in conflict with the Jewish community. Saint Augustine interpreted the parable the Good Samaritan (Luke 10:29-37) in the following way: the injured man is Adam; Jerusalem is paradise; Jericho is the world; the robbers are enemies; the priest is the Law of Israel; the Levite is the prophet; the Samaritan is Christ; the inn is the church. According to Augustine, the Jewish tradition is unreliable, while the church is the haven for those brought there by Christ.

Later, the missionary preaching incorporated elements of the new social context in its allegorizing in order to present the gospel message in an understandable manner to those of a different culture. This is known as the inculturation of the gospel. For example, many Latin American theologians used the suffering and exploitation the people were forced to endure as a window to understand God's gracious deliverance of the people in Egyptian bondage (Exodus). Allegory was also used in many of the theological controversies that arose within the church itself, as can be found in some of the church statements. Pope Innocent III (1198–1216) further developed Paul's allegorical comparison of Sarah and Hagar to point out the fate of their respective sons. According to him, Christians were destined to be free, while Jews were cursed as slaves.

Allegory provided a way of reading the Bible in a more-than-literal sense. It suggested that there was a deeper spiritual meaning that could be uncovered through the use of creative techniques. Soon four major types of interpretation developed: the literal, the allegorical, the tropological or moral, and the anagogical or spiritual. A clever Latin phrase helped medieval students remember and understand these four types:

Littera gesta docet	—	The letter teaches what happened;
quid credas allegoria	—	allegory, what you believe;
moralis quid agas	—	the moral, what you do;
quo tendas anagogia	—	anagogy, where you are going.

The literal sense is the meaning expressed immediately and directly by the words of the passage. The allegorical sense understands words as metaphors that stand for something other than what the word literally means. The tropological sense represents the words in terms of virtues of the soul. The anagogical sense is directed toward the final realities of death, judgment, heaven, and hell. An example explaining these four levels is the classis interpretation of Jerusalem:

Literally, it is a city in Judea;
allegorically, it stands for the church;
tropologically, it represents salvation;
anagogically, it refers to heaven.

A second example interprets a parable from the Gospel of Matthew (Matt 13:44). There we read: "The kingdom of heaven is like a treasure buried in a field, which a person finds and hides again, and out of joy goes and sells all he has and buys that field." Literally, there is a treasure in a field; allegorically, the treasure is the Gospel: tropologically, the Gospel is the pattern for virtuous living; anagogically, the Gospel assures us heaven.

These four approaches defined biblical interpretation for several hundred years, until the time of the Reformation when it was replaced in the Protestant churches by a new form of literal reading. Yet the use of these creative techniques continues to be popular today in some spiritual writings.

Midrash

Midrash is a type of biblical interpretation developed by Jewish scholars. The name is derived from the Hebrew word that means "to search." This approach presumes that the biblical text possesses an inexhaustible store of meanings, and with careful study one can discover the best meaning for a particular situation. It pays close attention to the meaning of individual words and often uses one verse to interpret another. (Many evangelical preachers use a similar approach in their explanation of a biblical text.)

There are two major kinds of midrash: *haggadah*, which is the interpretation of narrative; and *halakah*, the interpretation of law or custom. The version of the history of the monarchy found in the books of Chronicles is considered by many scholars as a haggadic midrash of the account found in the books of Samuel. Both Paul and the author of Acts of the Apostles seem to have known a haggadic midrash on the Exodus tradition, for they both stated that angels delivered the Law to Moses (Gal 3:19; Acts 7:53). The burgeoning of laws that reached its height with the 613 precepts that were in force at the time of Jesus is an example of halakic midrash. Many of the conflicts that Jesus had with the Pharisees stemmed from halakic interpretation of the Law. Examples include the accusation against the disciples for plucking grain on the Sabbath (Matt 12:1-8) and the controversy regarding divorce (Matt 19:1-9). Though not widely considered a critical form of interpretation, adding to the biblical tradition is a very common approach among some people today who believe that the passage as it stands is incomplete.

Theological Interpretation

One of the principal accusations that the sixteenth-century reformers lodged against the Roman Church was its manipulation of the biblical message to justify some of its questionable practices. Reformers claimed that the church's interpretation was far from the meaning intended by the biblical authors. Rather than interpret the Scriptures through the lens of church tradition, reformers insisted that a return to the original meaning was required. This turn to the past was the beginning of what came to be known as the historical criticism movement. It was not until 1943 with Pope Pius XII's encyclical *Divino Afflante Spiritu* that the Catholic Church officially adopted the approach, which originated among scholars from the Protestant traditions. From that time on, there has been little denominational difference in the various ways Christians and some Jews engage in critical biblical interpretation.

Though many individuals continued to read the Bible for the spiritual benefits it might provide, historical criticism soon became the chief approach for most Christian churches. Some scholars, though, began to argue that the biblical text, like any other example of classical literature, did not need its author to explain its meaning. Clues for discovering that meaning could be found within the text itself. These scholars turned to methods of literary criticism for their interpretation of the Bible. Though historical criticism still reigns supreme in most circles, the value of various forms of new literary criticism is now being recognized.

Finally, contemporary cultural studies have alerted us to the social bias present in much of our interpretation. Since modern forms of analysis generally originated in Europe and North America, the perspective of those societies became the standard point of view for the rest of the world. Recently, scholars representing what were previously considered minority groups have produced insightful biblical interpretations from their own perspectives. Today we can find South African historical-critical commentaries, Asian literary studies, and feminist critiques, to name but a few. Each approach uncovers some of the riches hidden in the passage. Together they provide invaluable insights into the biblical tradition.

Summary

Through the ages the biblical tradition has been interpreted in many different ways. We find evidence of such interpretation within the Bible itself. The primary focus of this post-biblical interpretation was the biblical passage itself, not the author of the passage or the specific reader. Early interpreters seem to have been unconcerned with the human authors, content to regard God as the principal author of the Bible. Furthermore, though fresh ways of understanding the Bible grew up because of new social, political, and religious situations of the readers, aspects of these situations were not analyzed. Interest in the author and the reader would have to wait for the modern period. Until then, innovative approaches to understanding the message of the text proliferate.

Chapter 8

How Do We Do It?

Over the years many different ways of interpreting the Bible have developed. Today scholars organize them under three different categories, depending on the primary focus of the approach. While every method seeks to understand the meaning of the biblical text, some interpreters maintain that the primary meaning is the one intended by the original author. In order to discover that meaning, these interpreters believe they must reconstruct the world within which that author lived. They prefer what have come to be called author-centered methods. Other interpreters argue that a work of art, in this case literature, can stand by itself without consulting the artist, or author. These interpreters are interested in the world created by that piece of literature, and they believe it is there that its meaning will be found. They prefer text-centered approaches. Finally, still others hold that meaning is really determined as the reader makes sense of the elements within the passage. These interpreters are interested in the world that is formed as the reader engages the message of that passage. They prefer reader-centered approaches.

Any method of interpretation appears to be overly complex and theoretical to those who are not trained in the field. In many ways, this may well be the case. Yet interpretation is really a means of understanding some form of communication, and some degree of interpretation is often necessary even in simple conversation. In many instances generational and cultural differences must be clarified; languages must be translated and interpreted; facial expressions and physical mannerisms must be explained. We encounter this need for interpretation whenever we move out of the narrow confines of our own social location into a world that is even slightly different from ours.

Methods of interpretation attempt to explain how this might be done when reading the Bible. They offer ways of explaining how the human mind works when 1) it seeks to understand a piece of literature that originated at another time and within a different culture (author-centered approaches); or 2) it seeks to understand the internal workings of that piece of literature (text-centered approaches); or 3) it seeks to understand aspects of the act of reading itself (reader-centered approaches).

Author-centered Approaches

When we read the Bible, we must remember that it is first and foremost literature. This statement in no way challenges our belief that the Bible is the inspired word of God. Rather, it reminds us that the religious message, which we hold as inspired, was inscribed in human words in a range of written forms by culture-bound authors. Hence the ideas found in the passage and their manner of expression grew out of a particular historical, cultural setting. If we are to grasp the meaning intended by the author, we must understand it from within the world that produced it. Historical-critical analysis is an attempt to reconstruct that world, as far as such reconstruction is possible.

Text Criticism

The first step in analyzing a passage using historical-critical methods is determining the actual text to be examined. This process is called text criticism. Not a single manuscript that was actually written by the original authors exists today. What we have are fragments of copies written by later scribes. This is true of both the New and the Old Testaments. The earliest version of the complete Bible we possess can be traced back to about the fourth century CE. Today text experts compare these fragments in order to create a version that they believe is as close to the original as is possible. The discovery of ancient Christian writings near Nag Hammadi, Egypt, in 1945, as well as the 1947 discovery of the Jewish Dead Sea Scrolls in the Qumran library, provided scholars with new materials with which to revise their earlier work. This kind of scholarly endeavor not only results in newer and updated versions of the entire Bible but also shows that through the centuries the biblical message took many slightly different forms depending on the social context of the people copying, interpreting, and preserving the texts.

Since the average person does not read the Bible in the original languages, the next important step in text criticism is translation. It is important to remember that no translation is precise. Every language contains words, expressions, and nuances that cannot be exactly expressed in another language. When translating from one language to another, some of these specific characteristics of the original language might be lost. On the other hand, the language into which the text is being translated often supplies new ways of expression. For instance, there was no word in ancient Hebrew for "soul." That was a Greek concept. And so, in the early century before Christ, when the Jewish people came under the influence of Greek culture, the introduction of Greek ideas like the soul provided the Jewish people a new way of thinking about life after death.

The challenge of translation can also be seen in that languages do not all have the same sequence of words. For example, in English, the modifying pronouns precede the noun, as in the phrase "my covenant" (Gen 6:18). In Hebrew the pronoun is attached to the end of the noun (*bᵉrîtî*). An exact translation of that form would be "covenant my," a way of speaking that is foreign to English. The sequence is adjusted in translation because intelligibility in the new language is more important than word-for-word precision.

There are two basic approaches to translations. One is often referred to as "formal correspondence." It seeks a translation that is as close to the original as possible. Following these principles of translation, *ádelphoí*, the Greek word used by Paul to refer to the Roman Christians, is rendered "brothers." "Dynamic equivalence" describes the second method of translation. It seeks to capture the meaning intended by the author and carry that meaning into a new context. Since it is clear that Paul's instruction was meant for the Roman men and women alike, the word *ádelphoí* is frequently rendered "brothers and sisters."

There are strengths and weaknesses in both methods of translation. Some translations or versions are more fitting in certain situations than others. The reader may choose a biblical paraphrase or poetic version for personal prayer or reflection. The desire today to use inclusive language in prayer has prompted many to favor a dynamic equivalence rendering. On the other hand, serious biblical study requires a critical translation, regardless of any bias that might be detected in the original language. Still other considerations come into play when biblical passages are used in liturgical celebrations or other forms of public prayer. In those circumstances, the context and sensibilities of the present praying community are more important than purely historical or linguistic factors.

In such cases, a dynamic equivalent version might be preferred. This situation points out some of the differences between author-centered and reader-centered approaches.

Historical Criticism

Once a text has been chosen for analysis, historical criticism seeks to understand the original message of the passage by reconstructing the original situation that produced it. In order to accomplish this, it uses clues discovered within the passage itself as well as the findings of archaeology and comparative religions. The language found in the passage plays an important role in this endeavor. Key words and phrases like "covenant" or "reign of God" provide windows into the social, cultural, and theological worlds of the biblical people. Reference tools such as biblical dictionaries and encyclopedias, concordances or alphabetic indices of major words, lexicons, and other word study books all provide invaluable information regarding those words and phrases that might be foreign to the contemporary reader but are found frequently in the biblical text. They help us reconstruct that ancient world.

The form and style of the biblical languages also help us to date the work, even when the content of the passage might suggest a different dating. This leads scholars to believe that the first account of creation (Gen 1:1–2:4a), with its emphasis on the establishment of an orderly universe out of cosmic chaos ("the earth was a formless wasteland, and darkness covered the abyss" [Gen 1:2]), originated during the Babylonian exile. At that time, the nation was itself engulfed in political, social, and theological chaos. The version of beginnings found in that account of creation would have inspired hope in the minds and hearts of a dispirited people, who themselves longed for an opportunity for a new beginning.

A firm grasp of the history of the ancient Near Eastern world serves as a backdrop for understanding the story of ancient Israel. The nations that thrived in the area known as Mesopotamia ("land between two rivers")—the Sumerians, the Akkadians, the Assyrians, the Babylonians, as well as the Egyptians in the Nile Delta area—all exerted significant influence across an area known as the Fertile Crescent. Since the land of Israel was located within that crescent, these ancient civilizations all left their marks on the people of Israel. We find Mesopotamian influence in the second account of creation (Gen 2:4b-25) and reference to Amenemope, an Egyptian scribe, in Proverbs (Prov 22:17–24:22).

In addition to these major powers, nations within the land of Canaan itself all figured in some way in the story of Israel. Such nations included the Amorites, the Hittites, the Moabites, the Edomites, and the Ammonites. One cannot reconstruct the history of ancient Israel without including details from the histories of these peoples. Many of their customs correspond to those described in the pages of the Bible. For example, both the close connection between the Israelites and the Edomites and the animosity that they shared is traced back to the story of the births of Jacob and Esau (Gen 25:19-34).

In like manner, knowledge of the history of the Mediterranean world during the first centuries of the Common Era will throw light on events that were important to and that shaped the early Christian communities. This history does not span as many centuries as does the history of Israel. Nor does it include as many other nations and civilizations. Nonetheless, one cannot adequately understand early Christianity without an appreciation of the Greco-Roman civilization and the impact that it made on the first followers of Jesus. Crucifixion, for instance, was a Roman punishment. Furthermore, many of the allusions found in Paul's writings are drawn from elements of the Greco-Roman culture, namely, his use of athletic imagery (1 Cor 9:24) and notion of savior as found in the Pastoral Letters (1 Tim 4:10).

Along with the histories of these ancient nations and civilizations, one must include knowledge of the geography of these lands. Their location in the ancient world and the specifics of the topography of the land sometimes afforded the people advantage and at other times resulted in disaster. Mountain settlements offered defense from invading enemies, while the fertile plains allowed the people to farm. Biblical atlases are invaluable sources of information in this regard.

Social-scientific Criticism

A form of historical criticism known as social-scientific criticism has gained prominence in the recent past. It examines the social and cultural aspects found within the passage. While historical criticism focuses on national matters, governments and relations with other nations, social and religious movements, and so forth, social-scientific criticism is interested in how social reality affected individuals. Based on the principle that all knowledge is socially conditioned and develops out of a particular perspective, this approach seeks to uncover that perspective. It studies how social systems are organized and how they operate, how social values are shaped and how they function, and how religious beliefs are developed, preserved, and handed down. Historical criticism asks questions such as: Who? What? Where? When?

Social-scientific criticism concentrates on questions such as: How? Why? For what purpose?

Social-scientific criticism begins with an identification of "social location." This phrase refers to the combination of several factors that constitute an individual's personal profile. These factors include gender, age, race, ethnic origin, economic class, level of education, political and religious affiliation, group membership, and location in place and time. Our own social location is integral to our experience and understanding. Because it is so much a part of our understanding reality, we usually presume ours to be the norm for all people, until we encounter a social reality dissimilar from our own. It is then that we become aware of differences in various cultural realities.

We should recognize this socio-cultural difference when we read the Bible, lest we interpret the cultural details found within its pages according to our own cultural models. We must remember that all of the biblical writings come from an ancient prescientific world that had Eastern characteristics, rather than a modern philosophical one with Western characteristics. This is particularly true with regard to such issues as gender identity and relationships, kinship and family patterns and traditions, social customs and organization, economic systems and structures, and military and political practices. Aspects of these and other social matters are embedded in biblical passages. Careful social-scientific analysis will uncover them, thus enabling the critic to reconstruct the social reality of the respective historical periods.

In order to accomplish its goal, social-scientific criticism utilizes the presuppositions, theories, and methods of the social sciences: cultural and social anthropology, sociology, economics, political science, cultural studies, as well as linguistics and the principles of communication. What this approach discovers by using methods from these areas demonstrates how the message found within the biblical text both reflects the social setting uncovered through this examination and responds to it. Only by examining the social characteristics of the biblical expression will we be able to grasp the religious meaning intended by the author.

An example might illustrate this. In Exodus we find the description of the establishment of covenant by God with the people of Israel (Exod 20:2-17). A study of treaty forms of the ancient Near Eastern world reveals an ancient Hittite formula quite similar to elements found in the Exodus passage. This historical information has thrown light on the meaning and function of the covenant as it was probably understood in ancient Israel.

Literary Criticism

Just as historical criticism is concerned with the historical circumstances within which the passage was written, so literary criticism is concerned with the passage as a piece of writing. It looks for clues to its meaning within the literary piece itself. Literary criticism has been understood in three major ways. First, the interpretive approach originated in the seventeenth century as the straightforward study of the Bible as literature. Today that dimension of the approach is known as source criticism. Second, during the twentieth century literary criticism sought to discover the meaning of the passage intended by the original author through a careful literary analysis of the various aspects of that passage. Third, today literary criticism employs the methods of modern literary theorists who show no interest in the original author, community, or intent. This approach is often referred to as new literary criticism.

The first way of understanding literary criticism will be discussed below under the heading "Source Criticism." The third way will be treated later in the section entitled "Text-centered Approaches." What follows is an explanation of the second way of understanding literary criticism, namely, as the analysis of the literary aspects of the passage in order to discover the meaning intended by the author.

The first step in this kind of literary criticism is the determination of the limits of a given passage. Identifying its beginning and its end determines its placement in the broader literary unit. This placement plays an important role in determining the way the passage functions within the broader unit. The form, structure, and style of the unit are then identified. As with all historically oriented approaches, it is important to discover what these features meant to the author or editor, not what they might mean to today's readers. Since literature is an inscribed form of communication, characteristics of the language—grammar, syntax, verb forms, and vocabulary—must be considered if the reader is to grasp the message intended. Several literary subgenres must also be analyzed, subgenres including hyperbole, metaphor or simile, symbolism, personification, and irony. All of these techniques communicate messages in unique ways, and the interpreter must know how they function in order to uncover the meaning of the message.

Narrative units require a specific type of literary analysis. Here the critic must attend to the structure and flow of the plot, the portrayal and development of characters, and the introduction and resolution of narrative tension. Distinctions must be made between narratives that are clearly historical in nature and those that are fictive or meant to teach a lesson. Literary critics must also be attuned to the perspective of the writing. Does the author want the reader to be sympathetic, unsympathetic, or even neutral toward certain characters in the story? This latter aspect indicates the way the narrative is meant to function in the mind and heart of the reader.

Form Criticism

Form criticism is the analysis of the literary types or genres employed in human communication. These forms fall into two major categories: prose or poetry. Prose includes such forms as myths, legends, folktales, historical accounts, gospels, epistles, miracle stories, and other narratives. Poetry includes hymns, psalms, prophetic oracles, and wisdom writings. Form criticism examines the relations of a specific genre to its historical setting, an oral tradition to its written expression, the literary form to its content, and typical forms to what is unusual in the passage.

The form-critical approach begins with the identification of the genre or conventional literary form of a passage, such as a law or a parable. It then seeks to discover the "situation in life" (German: *Sitz im Leben*) out of which or for the purpose of which the genre developed. The life setting of a legal statement was probably the law court, while that of a parable was a teaching situation. Knowing both the form and its life setting enables the critic to understand how the passage was meant to function within its specific literary context. This approach's concern for the form's "situation in life" demonstrates its interest in the community as a formative influence in shaping and preserving the biblical material, rather than simply seeing it as the work of an individual author.

Scholars agree that the biblical text is derived from an *oral tradition*. The transmission of this tradition from generation to generation resulted in the development of a number of layers of tradition, each layer possessing a particular meaning. These layers of tradition reflect the theological concerns of each generation. The oldest layer would be the original historical tradition consisting of a saying or an account of an event that probably took place in an actual experience. Each retelling of the tradition might bring further interpretation, until there could be several meanings attached to each other. Finally, the tradition was incorporated into a written account. The one who incorporated the tradition inevitably had particular theological reasons for doing so, reasons that might conceal the original meaning of the tradition.

The best example of this growth of tradition might be the development of a gospel. It would begin with oral tradition. The words of Jesus originated with Jesus himself. These sayings of Jesus were then handed down by word of mouth from one early Christian preacher to the next, who always adjusted the sayings to the needs and concerns of their audiences. They were then collected and incorporated into written gospel accounts. The authors came to be known as evangelists, from the Greek word for "good news."

A close connection exists between form criticism and other historical-critical approaches. First, form criticism is a type of literary criticism. This critical approach works its way through the many layers of the developed tradition in order to discover its original meaning and life setting. Thus it opens the door for a social-scientific examination. Reconstructing the process of tradition development from the original form to its final form is the task of tradition criticism. Finally, each of these approaches serves the goals of historical criticism.

While form criticism is usually employed in the examination of small units, it can also be used in the study of entire books. Both the book of Daniel and the book of Revelation are apocalypses, a creative form that describes the battle between the forces of good and the forces of evil. As such, these books can be analyzed for their form, content, and function. This does not mean that there might not also be other genres in these books. It simply means that the book itself can be classified as a particular genre.

Source Criticism

Source criticism, originally known as literary criticism, is the oldest form of modern critical biblical analysis. It claims that some of the contradictions, repetitions, and changes in literary style and vocabulary found in the Bible are evidence of different sources that have been gathered together to comprise the text as we have it today. We see this in the two different accounts of creation found in Genesis (Gen 1:1–2:4a; 2:4b-25), which are attributed to the Priestly and the Yahwist sources respectively (see "Postexilic Israel" in chap. 1). In the New Testament, the Gospel of Mark and a collection of sayings of Jesus referred to as Q (from the German *Quelle* or "source") are considered two of the primary sources for the Gospels of Matthew and Luke.

Source criticism challenges the theory of single authorship. In other words, the Documentary Hypothesis provides evidence disputing the claims that Moses wrote the Pentateuch (the first five books of the Bible). Careful source analysis challenges the notion that David wrote the Psalms, and that the gospel writers were eyewitnesses of the accounts in the life of Jesus that they recorded. It suggests, instead, that at times the individuals we consider the biblical authors functioned more as editors or creative reinterpreters of earlier traditions than as actual independent authors.

The goal of source criticism is threefold: to identify the literary components of the passage; to uncover the historical setting within which the tradition was composed; and to lay the groundwork for redaction criticism, which examines the process of tradition development itself. With few exceptions, the actual sources no longer exist, since they have been reinterpreted and incorporated into later editions. For this reason, the findings of source criticism have often been challenged. Where earlier critics claimed that the sections of the biblical material that they could identify as sources were actual literary fragments of earlier works, today critics may recognize the same features in the documents, but they question whether the material was handed down in literary form or in some traditional oral form. This questioning does not invalidate the approach of source criticism. Rather, it refines it. All scholars agree that there were sources; they disagree as to the form of those sources.

The most obvious exception to this uncertainty in identifying the findings of source criticism is found in the composition of the books of Chronicles in the Old Testament. These books clearly contain a reinterpretation of stories first recorded in the books of Samuel and Kings. Unlike other works examined by source criticism, both the sources (Samuel and Kings) and the later composition (Chronicles) are available for examination. A comparison of these two versions of this time in Israel's history shows quite clearly the editorial work done by the Chronicler and the revised perspective of Israelite monarchy that resulted from it.

Redaction Criticism

Redaction criticism seeks to discover the intended purpose of the final author or editor of a book. It accomplishes this task by investigating the way smaller units from either the literary or the oral tradition are put together to form larger units. It is interested in determining why these units were modified, connected, and arranged as they were. Its particular focus is the interaction between the earlier tradition and the concerns of later communities as the tradition was handed down from one generation to the next. In other words, it is interested in the various stages of editorial reinterpretation that are evidenced within the passage itself. Since redaction criticism is based on comparison, it can be employed only where a text reflects the use of an earlier tradition. Furthermore, rather than attempt a harmonization of disparities in the text, redaction criticism actually employs these disparities in order to uncover the various levels of editorial reinterpretation.

Unlike form criticism, from which it emerged, redaction criticism does not examine the various parts of the biblical unit in order to determine their original forms. Rather, it directs its attention to the ways the editors shaped and molded the material that they received, thus expressing their own theological concerns. Though this approach recognizes the editorial work of the various redactors, it considers these editors more than "scissor and paste" writers. Redactors are respected as creative theologians who were unwilling to relegate older traditions to the past, but who chose instead to reinterpret their theological sources and hand them down to address the pressing needs of their own community.

By examining the repetition of common motifs and themes as well as vocabulary and style, and by comparing two accounts of the same story, redaction criticism is able to detect the editorial activity of the redactor, which throws light on the needs and concerns of the community from which and for whom the works were composed. This process also shows that the narratives in the Bible are primarily concerned not with the exact chronological accounts of historic events but with the theological meaning of those accounts.

Redaction critics distinguish between what the characters *in* the passage are saying and what the editor *through* that passage is saying. In other words, they are interested in what the final author of Judges might have been emphasizing by telling the stories of the judges the way they are told. Likewise, in Luke's gospel, the sermon that included the Beatitudes was given "on a stretch of level ground" (Luke 6:17-23), while in Matthew it was given on a mountain (Matt 5:1-12). Scholars maintain that this was another example of how the author of Matthew's gospel sought to depict Jesus as a kind of second Moses, who himself delivered a way of life received on a mountain (Exod 19:20).

Strengths and Limitations of Author-centered Approaches

The goal of biblical interpretation is the personal transformation of the reader, not merely the acquisition of interesting information. While the Bible is certainly an anthology of various forms of literature, believers maintain that it is more than that. They hold that the Bible is the inspired word of God and, therefore, the primary source of divine revelation. Through the centuries, various methods of interpretation were developed and employed in order to avail the community of that revelation.

Despite the value of many of these approaches, the most recent official statement of the Pontifical Biblical Commission, entitled *The Interpretation of the Bible for the Church* (1994), identified the historical-critical method as the principal interpretive approach for today.

Since the biblical text is historical in origin, it is only right that interpretation should seek to reconstruct that origin in order to discover the text's earliest meaning. Historical-critical approaches all have some aspect of that discovery as their goal. Perhaps its greatest value is in its ability to set limits over the myriad of fanciful interpretations that were produced by earlier methods. Although we have no original copy of the Bible, rigorous text criticism establishes as the basis of all interpretations a version that is as close to that original text as we can get at this time in history. Study of the original language helps us to recognize the play of words found in so many places in the Bible. For example, in the second creation narrative the man (*ʿādām*) is made from ground (*ādāmah*), and the woman (*ʿishsha*) is built from the man (*ʿish*). These puns help us realize that the stories of the creations of the man and of the woman are poetic accounts and not historical or biological descriptions.

Historical criticism helps us place the events described in the biblical text within the broader context of the ancient Near Eastern or Greco-Roman worlds. It grounds these events in the real world of history. The crucifixion of Jesus is mentioned in the writings of the Roman historian Tacitus. This reference assists in refuting the claim posed by some detractors that Jesus did not really die and, therefore, could not have risen from the dead.

Social-scientific criticism consists of a comparative study of the social and political mores and practices of the Near East, of which ancient Israel was a part, and the Greco-Roman world of early Christianity. From this study we come to understand the levirate law that states that a man must take his deceased brother's widow as a wife and raise the child of that union as the heir of the deceased brother. This explains why Tamar was not condemned for tricking her father-in-law into impregnating her, and why, instead, Jacob was faulted for not seeing that a man of his family fulfilled the levirate obligation (Gen 38).

The study of parallel composition, a feature of literary criticism, reveals some of the theological differences of the Synoptic Gospels. In Matthew's account of the temptations of Jesus, the devil's suggestion that Jesus throw himself from the parapet of the temple is the second of three challenges (Matt 4:1-11). It is the third and last challenge in Luke's version (Luke 4:1-13). Scholars hold that this is an example of how the author of Luke's gospel frequently ends his story in Jerusalem, the city that functions in this gospel as the linchpin holding together the events in the life of Jesus and of the early church.

An appreciation of the various literary forms or genres and the way they function is invaluable in understanding the meaning of the passage being read. It will prevent us from reading imaginative poetry as if it were historical prose, the mythological creation narratives as if they were scientific accounts, and the apocalyptic visions in Revelation as if they were predictions of future events.

Source criticism explains the similarities as well as the differences found in the gospels of Matthew, Mark, and Luke. The similarities help identify the sources; the differences often suggest distinctive theological emphases. In the past, some interpreters wove episodes from all of the gospels into one harmonized story of the life of Jesus, thus obliterating the specific theology of the respective episodes. Source criticism avoids this interpretive mistake.

The theological emphases uncovered by source criticism can be traced and identified by means of redaction criticism. It moves the interpretation beyond consideration of the content of the biblical stories to an appreciation of the theological meaning within their specific context. In highlighting the distinct theology of four gospels rather than one harmonized story, redaction criticism reveals the spiritual wealth of our biblical tradition.

It is clear from this short overview that the historical-critical method has much to recommend its diligent use. Yet regardless of the strengths of each of these interpretive approaches, there are also limitations. In fact, the major limitation lies at the heart of its essential strength, namely that historical approaches focus on the time of origin of a passage, the history of its development, or the time of its canonical designation. They do not address the socio-political or religious context or needs of the contemporary community. For this to take place, a hermeneutical step must be taken. This limitation does not negate the inestimable value of the historical-critical approaches. It simply indicates that such analyses must be supplemented by other approaches.

Text-centered Approaches

"Formalism" is the general term frequently used to cover the broad category of approaches that concentrate exclusively on the passage's literary composition. It claims that the literary work is an object in its own right, standing on its own merits without any reliance on either the author or the reader. It studies the form of the passage rather than its content. It developed in reaction to methods that interpreted texts by relating them to matters that were extrinsic to the text, such as historical circumstances or emotional responses. Approaches to literary interpretation classified as "formalist" concentrate on what they consider the objective interplay and relationships between the passage's literary features. They also claim that the methods used in these approaches are themselves objective. These methods include literary criticism itself, structuralism, canonical criticism, and narrative criticism.

New Literary Criticism

Historical-critical scholars have long recognized the literary character of the Bible. Yet their interest in biblical literature is fundamentally historical. Historical critics asked such questions as: What was the ancient form of the passage? How did that form function in the world of the author or editor? Sometime in the 1960s this literary interest took a significant turn away from historical issues. Influenced by the findings of new literary criticism, some critics became interested in the final literary form of the passage itself, rather than its historical development or reconstruction. They maintained that understanding the literary styles, patterns, and techniques operating within the passage did not require information that was external to the Bible. They argued that meaning is to be found in the text itself rather than in the historical world of the author or editor. These new literary critics moved from examination of author-centered to text-centered approaches.

Text-centered approaches are synchronic, while the various forms of historical criticism are diachronic. "Diachronic" comes from the Greek *dia* meaning "through" and *chronos* meaning "time." It means "over time" or "historically." "Synchronic" comes from two Greek words, *syn* meaning "together with," and *chronos* meaning "time." Thus the word means "at the same time" or "simultaneous." Synchronic analysis is a vertical form of analysis, examining every aspect of reality in and of itself apart from historical progression or development.

While historical criticism might say that biblical literature is meant to describe or illustrate some religious point, new literary criticism argues that the purpose of literature is the simple pleasure of the literature itself. Historical criticism views the biblical text as a window through which one might view the community for which the message of that passage was originally intended. In contrast, new literary criticism considers the literary piece to be a mirror that reflects the world sketched within the passage, a world into which the reader is invited to enter. This shift in perspective does not negate the insights gained through historical-critical approaches. Rather, by disengaging the meaning of the passage from the limitations of one historical context (its original content), it broadens the scope of possible interpretations.

Reading the Bible primarily as literature rather than as religious proclamation does not diminish in any way its revelatory value. It is still considered the "word of God." It simply means that a significant shift in understanding the message of the Bible has taken place. We must remember that this shift to a literary reading is not the first shift in understanding the Bible that has taken place, though it is a significant one for the contemporary reader. The first shift occurred when the ancient Israelites gathered some of their traditions together because they believed that God was revealing something to them through those traditions. A second shift came about when the followers of Jesus interpreted those same traditions through a Christian lens. Using historical-critical methods to analyze the Bible constituted yet a third shift. The contemporary reading of the Bible as literature is merely a more recent move.

Each interpretive method, regardless of its specific approach, attempted to answer the same question: "What does the Bible mean?" Various answers to that question flowed from each of the shifts that took place. The first shift revealed the ancient Israelites' realization that God was actively involved in their everyday lives. The second shift testified to the Christian conviction that Jesus provided a new way of living in this world. The historical-critical shift produced insight into the original religious message of the text. Today, appealing to imagination and intuition, new literary criticism invites readers into an aesthetic experience that can lead to truth.

While many of the interpretive techniques employed by this form of literary criticism are the same as those used by historical criticism's literary analysis, the underlying presuppositions of these two approaches are quite different. First, historical-critical literary criticism maintains that the various literary forms arise out of specific historical settings and they find their meaning in those same settings. For example, law forms grew out of legal settings and are best understood within those settings. On the other hand, new literary criticism argues that a literary piece is fundamentally metaphoric rather than historic in character, and knowledge of history is not required for comprehension. One can be quite ignorant of life in medieval England and yet be captivated by

Shakespeare's classic play *Romeo and Juliet*. The structure of the play, the movement of its plot, and the development of its characters all find their meanings within the play itself.

According to new literary criticism, a text is a network of elements and structures in relationship to each other. Pieces fit together to create a unified whole. An analysis of a literary composition examines each individual element of that composition as well as its place and function in the whole. In this way, the poetic character and function of the text is examined. Unlike the historical-critical approach to form criticism, which is interested in the original setting and function of the literary piece, this kind of form criticism pays attention to the form itself and how it might function in various settings.

An example might demonstrate this. Hearing the parable of the tenants who took control of a vineyard and even put to death the heir of that vineyard (Matt 21:33-46), the early Christians would have identified those tenants as the religious authorities who were in power at the time of Jesus. On the other hand, literary critics today would not be limited by historical constraints. They would consider that parable a warning to any kind of leader who might forget that leadership is a sacred trust and not a personal entitlement, and that it can be taken away if it is not exercised for the sake of others.

Besides parables, contemporary literary critics examine various other literary forms found in the Bible. These are: myths, which are imaginative narratives that express profound truths (creation accounts, Gen 1–3); legends, meant to edify by telling stories about extraordinary people (stories about Samson, Judg 13–16); folktales, which explain an aspect of the people's culture (the explanation of Jacob's change of name, Gen 32:23-33); historical accounts, such as the stories of the Maccabean revolt (1 and 2 Maccabees); gospels, collections of stories about Jesus containing theological meaning and testifying to the faith of the early Christians (Matthew, Mark, Luke, John); miracle stories, which demonstrate the power of God at work in the lives of people (the raising of Lazarus, John 11:1-44); epistles, containing correspondence to a particular community of believers intended for instruction (the letters of Paul); psalms, which are poetic prayers expressing such religious sentiments as praise, hope, repentance, gratitude, and so forth (Psalms); prophetic oracles, either statements of warning or encouragement that call people to fidelity to their covenant commitment (Isa 40:1-3; Amos 2:6-16); and wisdom writing, containing maxims that provide insight into life (Prov 1:8-19).

New literary criticism also examines literary techniques: metaphor, allegory, hyperbole, euphemism, and personification. A metaphor is a figure of speech in which some aspect of one object is applied to another object as if it belonged to the second object, thus suggesting some kind of comparison. In the phrase, "His eyes are like doves" (Cant 5:12), the eyes of the beloved are compared to the innocence and gentleness of a dove. An allegory is a figurative piece in which the surface meaning carries another deeper meaning. As mentioned earlier in chapter 7, Paul claims that Sarah and Hagar represent the Jewish and Christian communities respectively: "Now this is an allegory. These women represent two covenants" (Gal 4:24).

Hyperbole is a form of exaggeration meant to make a point. It was used by the gospel writer who claimed "Jerusalem, all Judea, and the whole region around the Jordan were going out to [John] and were being baptized by him in the Jordan River" (Matt 3:5-6). A euphemism is a metaphorical expression used in place of a more precise word or expression that is considered offensive. Biblical writers frequently referred to "feet," rather than describe exposed sexual organs ("[Ruth] stole up, uncovered a place at his feet, and lay down" [Ruth 3:7]). Personification is a figure of speech in which human characteristics are ascribed to nonhuman reality. In the wisdom tradition, Wisdom itself is personified as a woman: "Wisdom has built her house" (Prov 9:1).

These are merely samples of some of the many techniques examined by means of new literary criticism. They are all metaphoric in some way and their imaginative character must be understood if one is to grasp their potential for meaning.

Structuralism

Structuralism is based on the conviction that the human mind functions in certain ways called structures. The approach originated in the nineteenth century in the field of linguistics or language structure, but it was fully developed only around 1957. Linguistics makes a distinction between competence in speech and the actual language system. This distinction is clear in young children who may be able to pronounce some words, but who have not yet fully grasped the underlying structure of the language itself.

Every language is a system of signs, and these signs are a combination of the "signifier" (the sound of the word or its written form) and the "signified" (the object to which it points). Signifier and signified are sometimes referred to as "expression" and "content." There is a necessary relationship between expression and content: the word "cat" is meaningless without an actual cat, and the cat is made comprehensible by means of the word in context. At the same time, the relationship between the expression and the content is also arbitrary. The animal is called "cat" in English, but *chat* in French and *popoki* in Hawaiian. The language system determines the appropriate signifier or expression.

A language is meaningful only if there is an appropriate relationship between the various structural elements of that language. Language possesses two basic kinds of relationships. One consists of order and sequence, such as the relation between subject and predicate, predicate and direct object, and modifying clauses. While this order is standard within a language, it differs among languages. In English, the possessive pronoun precedes the word it modifies; in Hebrew, the pronoun is a suffix of the word. The other relationship is between words that are either similar or contrasting. The first relationship includes objects that belong to the same category, such as wrens, sparrows, and robins. The second relationship includes such contrasts or binary opposites as life/death, up/down, good/evil, in/out, old/young. According to structuralism, we grasp the meaning of an object by recognizing its relationship with other objects, whether that relationship is one of similarity or opposition.

Closely related to structuralism is semiotics, from the Greek word *sēmeíon* (sign). In semiotics the sign is the fundamental building block. This field of investigation studies the relationships between signs in order to determine how meaning is constructed. While linguistics probes the structure of language, semiotics broadens the meaning of sign to include other manifestations of reality. For example, red has become the international sign for hot water, while blue signifies cold.

In the 1960s, anthropologists began to employ the principles of semiotics in the study of various cultures. Just as elements of a language make sense within the relationships or structure of that language, so elements of a culture make sense within the relationships or structures of that culture. For instance, in most contemporary societies, one marries outside of the extended family, while in societies like ancient Israel, one married within the extended family. In each situation, the social system as a whole gives meaning to the particular custom.

Structural analysis has become influential in the study of literature, and it is in this way that it has been adopted by some biblical critics. The same principles that govern the examination of language are employed in the examination of literary forms. Though here there is great diversity of literary form (narrative, wisdom maxim, psalm), structuralism maintains that this diversity becomes apparent in the actual written or spoken expression. These written or spoken forms are considered surface structures. In addition to diverse surface structures, there are patterns known as deep structures, which are abstract intuitions about how reality is to be structured. According to structuralism, authors unconsciously utilize these deep structures in their writing. Furthermore, it is these structures that carry the deep system of convictions in which the passage is grounded.

The first people to apply the principles of structuralism to biblical texts were, not biblical scholars, but linguists who were interested in the structure of the Hebrew language. There were also literary critics, who recognized the literary character of the Bible, and anthropologists, who were fascinated by ancient kinship structures found in biblical narratives and laws. These scholars may have been believers, but their primary interest was not theological.

Structural analysis begins with the identification of the form of the entire unit. Is it a myth? A prophetic oracle? A gospel? This is followed by an analysis of the various movements within the passage. The two standard movements within narratives are:

1) sender → object → receiver, and
2) helper → subject ← opponent.

The reader must then discover what changes occurred in these transactions. Analysis will reveal which of these changes were really transformative and, therefore, have deep symbolic value. Up to this point the analysis of the passage has been simply on the literary level, or on the way the passage has been organized. The next step moves the reader from that level to the level of symbolic meaning. It is at this level of symbolic meaning that one uncovers the deep convictions that underlie the text.

A classic example of this approach is the analysis of the story of Jacob's wrestling with the angel (Gen 32:23-33). What follows is a brief explanation of a structural analysis. It addresses only the major movements found within the passage. A more complete analysis would examine such obvious contrasts as night/day, blessing/injury, human/divine, or the importance of changing Jacob's name to Israel and naming the place Peniel.

Identification: heroic tale.
Movement 1:   A mysterious man attacks Jacob but cannot prevail against him.
Change: Jacob is seen as a hero.
Movement 2:   The mysterious man strikes Jacob's hip.
Change: Jacob now limps.
Movement 3:   Jacob demands a blessing.
Change: Jacob receives a change of name, which indicates that he has withstood divine power.

The first two movements correspond to features of a typical heroic tale (helper → subject ← opponent movement) in which a hero encounters a life-or-death threat and emerges victorious, though not without some degree of injury. In this tale, however, there is no helper. Given the broader context of the Jacob narratives, one would expect that God would be the helper, though this is not the case. The third movement is quite unusual. Jacob demands a blessing but receives a change of name.

This change of name is not a blessing but an explanation of what has just taken place. Israel, the name he is given, is derived from two Hebrew words, the verb *śārâ* (I contend with) and the noun *ʿēl* (the generic word for god). The name indicates that the one who attacked Jacob by the river was none other than the God from whom all blessings had originally come, the one the reader would have expected to be the helper. This is not only a twist in the hero tale but also a challenge to the conviction that a good God, one who promises blessings, would not be responsible for the hardship that comes into our lives.

This structuralist reading of the passage may not produce insights significantly different from those arrived at by another approach. Yet it does uncover the movements within the passage, and it does invite the reader to move more deeply into its meaning. Structuralism demonstrates well a text-centered approach to interpretation. It is an example of a form of analysis that examines every aspect of the passage apart from historical progression or development. Structuralism is interested only in the final form of the text. It shows that the intelligibility of the text can be found in its organization without any reference to the mind of the author.

Canonical Criticism

It is often difficult to classify canonical criticism. Some of the earliest critics to espouse its principles did not even consider it a type of criticism similar to form or redaction criticism. One might say that it is the final step in the historical-critical venture. But unlike the other historical approaches that limit themselves to the examination of small units, to the process of the development of the tradition, or to the earliest literary forms found in the passage, canonical criticism is concerned with the final form of the text. Furthermore, its interest is in that form not merely as final, but as the form accepted by the believing community that regarded it as authoritative.

Canonical criticism, though it can be classified as a text-centered approach, developed as a reaction against the text-centered insistence that the biblical text should be allowed to stand on its own. Canonical critics concede that this may be true when one is examining the Bible simply as literature, but believers argue that Scripture is more than literature. It is the inspired word of God that grew out of the faith of believing communities and has been interpreted as such through the ages. They insist that the legitimate context for interpreting the Bible is neither the original community alone nor the literary arrangement of the text but the current believing community.

For canonical critics the "situation in life" of the biblical passage is the present believing community, which is the heir to the communities that originated and developed the biblical tradition. In this respect, canonical criticism is similar to some of the reader-centered approaches that recognize the role played by the reader in interpreting the biblical text. Canonical critics argue that many of the historical approaches used to examine the Bible have undermined its religious integrity. Furthermore, since each biblical book belongs to the entire canon of inspired books, they maintain that no book should be read in isolation, but should be read along with the rest of the biblical books.

Canonical criticism has two major foci. The first is the complex historical canonical process that produced the Bible. The second is the use of the process in the interpretation of the text. The canonical process is based on the dynamics of the process of development of tradition. Biblical tradition is grounded in the belief that some aspect of God is revealed in human experience. A report or description of the revelatory event or realization is then handed on to others. If those who receive the report find that it helps them to understand something about God, they will make it their own and will hand it on to others. In this way, a tradition is born. As it is handed on, the tradition may undergo slight changes, so that those who receive it can accept it as their own.

An example will illustrate this. At one time in their history, the ancestors of the Israelites lived under Egyptian control. At a time when they were no match for the Egyptians, they were able to escape and establish themselves in the land of Canaan. They credited God for this escape and told the story of it to the next generation. This story soon became the founding story of the people and was handed down generation after generation. Details may have changed, but the basic story endured. Over the years, this process produced various versions of the story, each one addressing both its basic theological meaning and the needs and concerns of the community receiving the story. Eventually one version of the story became the standard version. At a much later time in history, the standard version became part of a much longer account of Israel's story. All of the major traditions were brought together into what has come to be known as the canonical text. The same process occurred in the formation and development of early Christian traditions, which were added to the canonical text to form the entire Bible.

This canonical process demonstrates the flexibility of the important traditions as they were adapted to new situations. The technique employed in adapting them is called resignification, or assigning new significance or meaning in new contexts. The traditions became stabilized only in the final phase of the process. Canonical critics maintain that even these stabilized or canonical traditions are flexible or adaptable. If this were not the case, we would never be able to interpret the Bible for our own day. The difference is not in the degree of the adaptability of the traditions but in the fact that new resignification does not become part of the canonical tradition. It is simply part of the history of ongoing interpretation.

Some canonical critics take this approach a step further and seek to discover the hermeneutical or interpretive techniques used by the biblical writers as they developed and reinterpreted the traditions. These critics argue that the idea of a biblical canon includes not only the final literary text but also traces of the interpretive approach that produced that text. They search the text itself for these traces. Like historical critics they study the traditions in order to discover how they developed. But while historical critics are interested in the historical significance of this development, canonical critics are interested in the literary steps involved in it. As mentioned above, it is clear that 1 and 2 Chronicles are reinterpretations of material found in the books of Samuel and Kings. Historical critics are interested in the reinterpretation and what it tells us about the community of the Chronicler. In other words: What did it mean? Canonical critics, on the other hand, are interested in the steps taken in the process of reinterpretation. They want to know: How did they do that?

The canonical approach contends that there are three major components that were operative during the process of tradition development: 1) the passage or text containing the tradition that is being handed down, 2) the new historical context within which the tradition is being reinterpreted, and 3) the technique of interpretation. That technique might be literal, allegorical, tropological, or anagogical as the medieval scholars employed; it might be more a comparative technique like the Jewish approach known as midrash, which is a metaphoric way of interpreting (see chap. 7). Regardless the technique employed, canonical criticism always reinterprets a cherished tradition in such a way that it will continue to be meaningful in a new context. Canonical hermeneutics searches for the traces of these approaches in order to employ them in providing an interpretation for the contemporary community.

Canonical criticism is considered a text-centered approach because it claims that the revelatory potential of the Bible is found in the final form of the tradition. It is not found, as author-centered approaches claim, in an earlier source or draft of the passage. It also requires that, like the many generations of believers before us, we attend to the character and needs of the community receiving the tradition if that tradition is to exert its potential for transformation of the community.

Finally, canonical critics uphold four important principles when interpreting biblical texts. First, there is an obvious ambiguity about reality that requires flexibility in the way we interpret that reality. Second, the biblical text should be considered a mirror for discovering something about ourselves, not as a model for us to imitate. Third, we must seek to discover the theology or the action of God described in the passage. Fourth, only then should we decide how our lives should conform to God's action.

Narrative Criticism

Narrative criticism is another text-centered approach that is interested in the narrative as narrative, not as a source of historical information about the author or the community for which the story was originally intended. It developed within the field of biblical studies, specifically for the examination of gospel stories. It differs from those text-centered approaches that claim that the meaning is found exclusively in the text. Rather, it maintains that meaning cannot be realized without a reader. It insists that every narrative has two aspects, an artistic aspect and an aesthetic one. The artistic aspect is credited to the author who created the narrative; the aesthetic aspect is ascribed to the reader who actualizes the message of the narrative.

Like structuralism, narrative criticism recognizes that narratives are signs that have both a signifier and a signified. The signifier is the narrative discourse, the signified is the content of the story—but only a reader can actualize the content of the story. It is not enough to analyze the structure and meaning of the parts of the story. One must also discover its purpose. Narrative criticism examines every aspect of a story in order to discover the effect that story is meant to produce in the reader. Historical literary criticism examines the literary elements of setting, plot, and character, but it does so in order to discover its original meaning. Narrative criticism is attentive to the reader. But which reader?

Rhetorical criticism is a historical approach that is interested in how the message affected the original reader, the one for whom the text was originally intended. Structuralism envisions a reader who can decipher the various literary codes within the passage. Narrative criticism speaks of an implied reader, one who will respond to the values and concerns woven into the story. As it seeks to make explicit the implicit dynamics that are operative when one reads, narrative critics identify six "persons"—the real author and the real reader, the narrator and the narratee, the implied author and the implied reader.

First there is the real historical author and the real historical reader. In reading, though, we know nothing about that real author. What we do know is a certain point of view, values, and concerns that are revealed in the narrative. This point of view is referred to as the implied author. In a sense, though created by the real author, this point of view or implied author exists only in the story. In like manner, the author is writing for a reader, but knows nothing about any real reader. But the author does have in mind a reader who will respond appropriately to the point of view contained in the story. This reader is called the implied reader. Like the implied author, the implied reader is found only in the story. Finally, every story has a narrator, whether that narrator is explicitly identified or not. It is the narrator who tells the story to a narratee, who also may or may not be identified.

The real author produces a text within which a story unfolds. One might say that the real author and the real reader live in their respective historical worlds, while the implied author and the implied reader are limited to the world created by the text. Finally, the narrator and the narratee are engaged in the dynamics of the world of the story. The world within that story may or may not resemble the real world, for what is important is the point of view revealed therein. It is this point of view that is meant to effect a change in the implied reader.

Since the average reader is accustomed to reading the biblical story as if it were an actual historical account, it might be better to use a different narrative to illustrate this. William Shakespeare will be the real author and any reader can be considered the real reader. An anonymous narrator tells the story *Romeo and Juliet* to an anonymous narratee. The story line of the drama recounts the tender blossoming of young love and then its tragic end. Yet the play is really about the pointlessness of longstanding prejudice and civic acrimony and the catastrophic consequences such a situation might produce. This is the point of view that comes to expression in the story. In other words, this point of view is a profile of the implied author.

Having been invited into the play, which is an artistic creation of the author, the real reader must now perform an aesthetic function by putting the story together in order to uncover its real meaning and to accept the challenge that it offers. There will be a highly subjective quality to this function because every reader is different and will fashion the aesthetic character of the story in a unique way. This fashioning is done by filling in the gaps that inevitably appear in every story. Having done that, the question remains: Will the reader accept the point of view intended for the implied reader and be transformed by it? This is the goal of narrative criticism. Though the reader plays an important role in narrative criticism, it is still considered a text-centered method of interpretation. This is because of the prominent roles played by the implied author and implied reader, and these two "persons" are found exclusively in the text itself.

From this summary of a reading of *Romeo and Juliet* one should have a good grasp of what happens when reading a gospel narrative. There, an ancient writer, under the guise of an eyewitness named John, tells a story of how some disciples walked away from Jesus (John 6:66-68). A believer, confronted by the challenge of the story, is faced with a comparable decision to accept the demands of Jesus or to walk away. In order to appreciate the character of the challenge, the reader must examine all of the elements of the narrative. These include: the setting and sequence of time, the movement of the plot, the depiction of the characters, and particularly the narrative techniques and patterns employed by the gospel writer. The meaning and function of these elements can be determined only by reading the entire gospel and in that way discovering the information needed to understand the passage under consideration.

Though there is great similarity in reading a play and reading a gospel, there is also a significant difference. In the case of the play, the values, concerns, and point of view are the author's. In the case of the gospel, which believers maintain is the inspired word of God, the values, concerns, and point of view are God's. Here again the role of the reader comes into play in the very act of reading, for it is the faith of the reader that provides the standard for judging the importance of the values and concerns portrayed in the story.

Strengths and Limitations of Text-centered Approaches

It was precisely the limitations of the historical-critical approach to biblical interpretation that gave rise to new literary criticism. This text-centered approach sought to remedy those limitations. Rather than dissect the passage and examine only its parts, new literary criticism considered the passage as a whole unit. This form of criticism understands literature as an inscribed form of communication and thus utilizes communication models of speech-act theory in its approach. Its most obvious strength lies in its rejection of an outside referent for discovering the meaning of the passage.

The primary opposition to new literary criticism is its claim to self-sufficiency. This claim poses two major problems. The first regards the nature of the Bible. Believers maintain that it is the inspired word of God. Thus its truth claims are legitimated by a standard outside of the text. The self-sufficiency of new literary criticism also denies the role played by the reader in the act of reading.

Perhaps the greatest strength of structuralism as a method of biblical analysis is its acknowledgment of human beings' innate structuring capacity. It maintains that insight into the way the human mind works will provide insight into ways of interpreting. This capacity limits possible interpretations to the boundaries set by the poles of the structure that has surfaced. The utilization of binary opposites in determining that structure opened the passage to areas for interpretation not covered by other methods.

Many critics argue that structuralism is a method turned in on itself. Furthermore, the structuralist examination of signs and symbols may function well in linguistic studies or in semiotics, but it must be adapted in the analysis of biblical narratives. In this latter case, one risks imposing rigid structures on fluid stories. Finally, since there are no criteria for deciding which binary oppositions to use, the character of the structuring pattern is quite arbitrary.

Like other text-oriented approaches, canonical criticism rejects historical criticism's claim that there is one primary meaning, insisting instead that the message of the Bible will touch different readers in various ways. Unlike some of the new literary critical approaches, it cherishes the biblical text as the inspired word of God and not merely as a literary text. While it is concerned with the biblical passage that has been handed down, it is also attentive to the needs of the present believing community.

Probably the most challenging aspect of the text-centered approach is the ambiguity regarding the nature of techniques of resignification. Techniques such as comparative midrash (creative comparison) have not been clearly defined, thus opening the interpretive approach to methods that lack specificity and rigor. This might lead to a return to precritical approaches to biblical interpretation.

Narrative criticism has much to recommend it. Most important, it invites the reader into the biblical text itself, there to be transformed by its dynamic message. Furthermore, this invitation is extended to the average reader and not merely to the expert, as is the case with rigorous historical-critical methods. The uninitiated reader may find the distinction between real and implied author and reader confusing, but that distinction is made only in the explanation of the dynamic of reading. It is not a step in the reading itself. If historical-critical methods dissect the biblical message, narrative criticism returns it to the community of believers. Finally, with its insistence on the prominent role played by point of view, narrative criticism enables the reader to discover the different perspectives created by each biblical author.

Despite these strengths, there are also drawbacks in the approach of narrative criticism. One of its major characteristics is also a limitation: it treats a gospel as if it were a coherent unit rather than a collection of separate stories. Furthermore, it examines the inspired biblical story with techniques devised to examine fiction. The reader must supply the faith dimension. Finally, narrative criticism's opposition to any claim of objective meaning can result in interpretations that are too subjective, or in too many subjective interpretations.

Reader-centered Approaches

Just as there is no text without an author, so there is no communication without a reader. According to reader-centered approaches, if there is to be any real meaning, the reader must engage in an interactive exchange with the text, not with the author of that text. In this exchange, aspects of the reader's own world of experience and understanding engage with issues found within the text. Meaning is then discovered and formulated in terms that make sense to the reader. This meaning may be quite different from that which one might expect from the author or original community. Despite this activity on the part of the reader, this type of interpretation is not simply a product of the subjective whim of the reader. To be authentic, a reader-centered interpretation should find its grounding within the literary parameters of the passage under consideration.

Reader-centered approaches include various techniques that stress the reader's role. Focus on the reader requires that the reader's social location be identified. This social location influences what is known as pre-understanding—a collection of presuppositions that the reader brings to the act of reading, presuppositions of which the reader may be unaware. Reader-centered approaches also include advocacy stances that may significantly influence the focus of one's reading. Finally, some contemporary interpreters engage in various other forms of deconstruction.

Reader-response Criticism

Like narrative criticism, reader-response criticism developed in opposition to the claims of new literary criticism and structuralism that the meaning of the text could be found exclusively within the text itself. It maintains that the meaning of a passage cannot be realized without a reader. In this way, reader-centered approaches are much like performance art. A play is not a play until it is performed; nor is a symphony a symphony. The same is true of a piece of literature. It must be read if it is to come alive. Furthermore, though the text speaks to the reader, the action moves in both directions. In other words, the reader engages the text in a way unique to that specific reader and thus actualizes the potential that resides in the text.

As with narrative criticism, reader-response recognizes both the artistic and the aesthetic aspects of literature. The artistic aspect is attributed to the author who created the narrative; the aesthetic aspect relates to the reader who actualizes the message in that passage. Like narrative criticism, reader-response is interested in that reader. Yet there are significant differences between these two interpretive approaches. Narrative criticism is concerned with the implied reader, a reader that is assumed within the text. Reader-response is interested in the real flesh-and-blood reader. Furthermore, while narrative criticism examines how the text focuses the reader's response, reader-response emphasizes the role of the reader in determining the meaning of the passage.

Reading engages the reader's imagination. The author provides the text, but the reader puts flesh on the characters, fills in the gaps in the narrative plot, and brings the story to life. This becomes clear when we remember our surprise when a character, whom we have envisioned while reading a story, appears quite differently in a movie version of that story. Since readers draw on their own imaginations and experiences in accomplishing the aesthetic task, and since imagination and experience are quite dissimilar among readers, the aesthetic product will differ from reader to reader.

This difference becomes evident in the way the reader fills in the gaps that are present in all writing. One human mind might move thoughtfully through the development of a thought or idea, while another human mind might intuitively skip from idea to idea. The gaps in the story could be inconsistencies, discontinuities, or ambiguities. Such gaps in communication can be addressed immediately when one is engaged in one-on-one conversation, but this cannot be done when gaps are encountered in reading. In the latter case, the reader corrects the inconsistencies, connects the discontinuities, and clarifies the ambiguities, thus contributing to the story and accomplishing the aesthetic dimension of reading.

As unique as this may be with different readers, there is no such person as a totally independent reader. All readers belong to societies that determine the way signs and words are to be understood. Therefore, despite certain individuality, every reader is limited in reading by the literary composition of the passage and by the social world of understanding of which that reader is a member. For instance, when an author mentions a character's family, is the reference to a nuclear family, as one finds in most Western societies? Or to an extended family consisting of more than one generation, as is found in more traditional social groups? Or to a religious organization in which members make a permanent commitment? Regardless of the reference intended by the author, unless there is more information in the text itself, the experience of the reader will influence how the word "family" is understood.

It is probably safe to say that most people read the Bible from some form of reader-response approach. They "fill in the gaps" present in the story. They might harmonize the discrepancies found in the two creation narratives (Gen 1:1–2:4a and 2:4b–25), or they might explain Mary's words to Jesus on the occasion of the wedding in Cana as an expression of concern for the newly married couple (John 2:3). Noncritical readers usually presume that the passage they are reading is an account of a historical event that actually occurred as it is reported in the biblical text. This means that they consider the additions they make to the story as enhancements of an actual historical report rather than aesthetic contributions in a reader-response form of interpretation.

This reader-centered approach recognizes the rhetorical character of literature, its ability to affect our emotions and influence our behavior. It examines, not the literary work itself, but how readers respond to that work. The examination of the text itself is the task of text-centered approaches. Reader-response acknowledges the potential for meaning present in the passage, but it asks the question: What is it about the reader that generates the meaning found in the passage? This characteristic of reader-response differentiates it significantly from structuralism. Structuralism insists that it is an objective approach, which can reveal meanings within the text that has little to do with the affective or emotional character of the reader. On the other hand, reader-response maintains that there is no such thing as objective reading. Only subjects read, and they read subjectively. While reader-response is based on the principle of affective response, strict text-centered approaches argue that such response is inconsequential and refer to this notion as the "affective fallacy."

The reader-response approach shares narrative criticism's interest in point of view; but where narrative criticism is interested in the implied author's point of view, reader-response recognizes what has come to be called the "wandering viewpoint" of the real reader. It claims that various points of view besides that of the implied author are open to the reader. This includes the point of view of the narrator, the narratee, and any one or all of the characters. Reading in this way opens the reader to a great variety of perspectives and insights. Gospel readers are often encouraged to read in this way, lest they always identify with the heroic characters and miss the challenge that is placed before other characters in the story.

Comprehension of a passage occurs when the horizon of the world within the texts is brought to bear on the horizon of the world of the reader. But what does this mean? Both narrative criticism and reader-response criticism speak of the implied author, or the ideological point of view consisting of the attitudes, values, and concerns revealed in the story. This point of view can also be considered the horizon of the world opened up by text. There is also the world of the real reader, a world with its own point of view, attitudes, values, and concerns. In reading, the language of the text is the medium that brings the horizons of these two worlds together. This fusion of horizons is not one of commonality, as would be experienced with whatever in the story might be familiar to the reader. Rather, it is one of self-transcendence, which occurs precisely when the reader faces some aspect of the unfamiliar. It is this encounter with the unfamiliar that accounts for the transformative character of the fusion of horizons.

Pre-understanding

Contemporary interpretive theory has made us aware of what it calls pre-understanding, which consists of various presuppositions that influence the way we understand what we experience or what we read. Contrary to a view held by many, there is no purely objective way of looking at things. We are not free of the heritage that has shaped our worldview. This heritage has predisposed our judgments, called forth our values, and actually shaped the way we perceive reality. The several cultures that each of us claims (religious, national, ethnic, political, etc.) have played a significant role in forming us into the people we have become. We possess many of the features of these cultures and we carry the effects of their histories. Though this pre-understanding is never fully self-conscious, it influences our thinking and our preferences.

Religious pre-understanding is shaped by the way we understand our respective faith traditions. It is not the faith tradition itself but the character of our understanding of that tradition. Frequently what we learned as children continues to influence our thinking. For instance, we may have been told that heaven is up above, a concept that corresponded well with the worldview of ancient Israel: "The LORD looks down from heaven" (Ps 14:2). Despite the fact that modern science provides us with a very different understanding of the universe, this earlier notion may still be part of the pre-understanding that operates in our thinking. We may still believe that heaven is up above us.

Religious pre-understanding often differs from faith to faith. Ancient Israel does not seem to have had a clear idea of life after death. We see this in the psalmist's plea for life and in the argument that God will not be praised if the psalmist dies:

> What gain is there from my lifeblood,
>   from my going down to the grave?
> Does dust give you thanks
>   or declare your faithfulness? (Ps 30:10)

The absence of belief in an afterlife affected the way the ancient Israelites viewed life itself. For them, the goal of life was a life well lived. On the other hand, the early Christians had been influenced by the Hellenistic notion of immortality. They believed in a life after this life, and this conviction influenced their way of thinking and living. This explains why Paul could say: "I long to depart this life and be with Christ" (Phil 1:23).

Finally, religious pre-understanding sometimes differs between Christian denominations. The interpretation of a particular passage in the Gospel of Matthew exemplifies this well. There we read that Jesus said to Simon Peter: "[Y]ou are Peter, and upon this rock I will build my church" (Matt 16:18). Roman Catholics hold that this line of authority can be traced from Peter to the present pope. They maintain that this particular passage should be seen as evidence of that religious conviction. While Protestants do not reject a literal reading of this passage, the splintering of the Christian community into several segments resulted in various ways of interpreting papal authority. Protestants do not believe authority should be exercised exclusively by the pope but, rather, that leaders of other denominations also enjoy some form of apostolic authority. One's denominational presumptions influence the way this passage is understood.

The national history of a people also fashions a form of pre-understanding. Some people interpreted the early expansion of the United States, known as "manifest destiny," in light of ancient Israel's occupation of the land of Canaan. Since the indigenous people were not Christian, their expulsion was often justified by an application of such passages as: "[T]here is a living God in your midst, who at your approach will dispossess the Canaanites" (Josh 3:10). The ferocity with which these indigenous people tried to defend their land and themselves was judged to be barbaric, and their extinction was thus justified. This mentality still exists in the minds of some people, and they read the Bible through this lens.

When people are living in a monocultural society, they may not be aware of how ethnic culture affects their thinking. With the influences created by globalization, however, it is difficult to find such a society in today's world. Still, our ethnic cultures often shape the way we interact with others, our favorite forms of entertainment, our choice of food, and so forth. Ethnic biases are quite common in multicultural societies, even societies that claim to be open to diversity. This can be seen in the spoken language, the preferred cultural practices, and the character of educational and occupational opportunities. People who have been pushed to the margins of one society are often the best ones to recognize comparable discrimination of another. They will feel the bite in Jesus' words when a Canaanite woman begged him to cure her daughter, and Jesus characterized her people as "dogs" (Matt 15:26). On the other hand, they will celebrate the diversity of tongues at Pentecost (Acts 2:8-11) in a way that those of the dominant group might not.

Because of their own national experience, many people associate slavery with race. Yet slavery is really a political abuse of power by one social group over another. In the United States the past enslavement of Africans still affects every dimension of society, despite the advances that have been made over the years. The same is not true in countries like Great Britain, though that country still struggles with the effects of colonialism. Because this political abuse has left its mark on the psyche of African-Americans, they recognize its characteristics wherever they may appear in the Bible. They will challenge any interpretation suggesting that blackness is a punishment for sin, as some readers in the past misunderstood the mark of Cain (Gen 4:15). They might point out that, in fact, the opposite is true, as seen in an account of Aaron and Miriam criticizing Moses for marrying a black woman. As punishment for her sin, Miriam was turned white with leprosy (Num 12:10). (Feminists will be troubled by the gender bias in this story, since Aaron also criticized his brother, but received no punishment.)

Finally, class figures prominently in one's social location. Though people usually think of class as an economic designation, it is determined by many more factors, including education, employment, or even physical ability. Racial, tribal, or ethnic identity can also influence one's class, as can gender identity. All of these factors have some bearing on class status. But unlike those other factors, class is not a permanent designation. It is possible to move from one class to another. Probably the most significant aspect of class is the power that is associated with it. Those who belong to the privileged class, determined by any one or more of the factors mentioned above, wield power over others.

Class plays an important role in the Bible as well, although in many passages the bias is in favor of those who do not have power. In ancient Israel's patriarchal society, the truly righteous person was the one who cared for those with no legal status in society, those who had no male protector. Three groups were singled out in particular: widows, orphans, and resident aliens (Deut 24:19). Disregard for class is found in the New Testament as well. There we find Jesus calling his followers to be like him, "meek and humble of heart" (Matt 11:29). Class still plays a role in the biblical stories, but both ancient Israel and the early Christian community turned class status upside down.

As stated above, our pre-understanding influences the way we experience and understand life. Therefore, it influences the way we read the Bible. It both provides us with insight into what is represented in the text and also limits our perception to aspects of our own life experience.

Reader-centered approaches to biblical interpretation call us to make as explicit as possible the implicit pre-understanding that flows from our social location so that we are aware of any predispositions we might bring to our reading.

Advocacy Approaches

Advocacy approaches are so named because they grow out of a commitment to some form of social justice. They advocate a political focus that takes remedying the oppression of the vulnerable as the starting point of interpretation. This approach first became known as it was promoted by Latin American liberation theology. It was then taken up by feminists, and has now been adopted by several other advocacy causes such as African-American, Hispanic, African, and Asian critiques, to name but a few.

An advocacy approach to reading the Bible has a twofold goal. First, it uncovers discriminating tendencies in the Bible itself. Second, it provides interpretations that both challenge current oppression and enhance the circumstances of those presently suffering. Sensitivity to the circumstances in the lives of oppressed and/or the marginalized people provides a point of view that can recognize traces of similar oppression or marginalization in the lives of biblical characters. Once this has been uncovered, the advocacy reader appeals to those passages that recount God's particular concern for the needy. One of the most obvious passages precedes the account of Israel's deliverance from bondage in Egypt:

> I have witnessed the affliction of my people in Egypt and have heard their cry of complaint against their slave drivers, so I know well what they are suffering. Therefore I have come down to rescue them. (Exod 3:7-8)

This story soon became the symbol of God's promise of liberation from other oppressive situations. In fact, Israel's return from Babylonian exile was seen as a second exodus:

> In the desert prepare the way of the LORD!
> Make straight in the wasteland a highway for our God! (Isa 40:3)

The exodus theme became the lens through which various oppressed people began to read the Bible. It was a favorite theme of the African people who were enslaved in the United States. The spiritual hymns that sprang from their faith continue to give evidence of this.

The New Testament also contains this message of liberation and fulfillment. This can be seen in the stories of the loving care that Jesus showed those who lived on the margins of society:

> The Spirit of the Lord is upon me,
>   because he has anointed me
>   to bring glad tidings to the poor.
> He has sent me to proclaim liberty to captives
>   and recovery of sight to the blind,
>   to let the oppressed go free,
> and to proclaim a year acceptable to the Lord. (Luke 4:18-19;
>   Isa 61:1-2)

Passages from Mary's song of praise, the Magnificat, also took their place next to the exodus story as a clarion call for justice:

> [God] has thrown down the rulers from their thrones
>   but lifted up the lowly.
> The hungry he has filled with good things;
>   the rich he has sent away empty. (Luke 1:52-53)

Advocacy reading of the Bible resulted in what has come to be known as the "preferential option for the poor." This principle, which reflects the words of Jesus: "Amen, I say to you, whatever you did for one of these least brothers [or sisters] of mine, you did for me" (Matt 25:40), was at the heart of the social teaching of Pope John Paul II and continues to shape the social teaching of the church.

The advancement of women, not only in the United States but also in many countries around the world, raised the consciousness of women and men alike to the discrimination to which women have been subjected in every aspect of their lives. Some people claim that the Bible itself relegates women to a position that is inferior to men. They appeal to the status of women in the patriarchal structure of biblical society as evidence of this. In response to this bias, feminist biblical interpreters remind us that the woman and the man were both created "in the divine image" (Gen 1:27) and thus have equal dignity regardless of the societal perspective from which most of the Bible was written.

The dignity of women is evident in various New Testament passages as well. Many of the followers of Jesus were women: "There were many women there, looking on from a distance, who had followed Jesus from Galilee, ministering to him" (Matt 27:55). The first witnesses to the resurrection were women: "Then they [the women] went away quickly from the tomb, fearful yet overjoyed, and ran to announce this to his disciples" (Matt 28:8). Finally, at Pentecost, the Spirit came upon all the believers, women and men, in fulfillment of the prophecy of Joel:

> "It will come to pass in the last days," God says,
>   "that I will pour out a portion of my spirit upon all flesh.
> Your sons and your daughters shall prophesy." (Acts 2:17; Joel 3:1)

Despite these and other similar passages, bias against women continues to be a troubling characteristic of the Bible. The biblical languages themselves are androcentric (male-centered). A passage quoted earlier is a good example of this: "Amen, I say to you, whatever you did for one of these least brothers [or sisters] of mine, you did for me" (Matt 25:40). Often both Hebrew and Greek passages contain words that are masculine in form but which are meant to include women in their meanings. Many people today argue that words such as "men" or "mankind" do not include women and should not be used as if they do. They insist that "men and women" or "humankind" better express inclusivity.

In addition to this problem with biblical language, interpreters sensitive to gender issues are often troubled by the way women are depicted in biblical stories. Most of those women seem important only because of their childbearing ability. While this role may be paramount in societies that are struggling for survival, such is not the case in most societies today. Despite this fact, biblical women are still held up as models to be emulated, thus reinforcing biased stereotypes.

Actually, it is neither the language nor the depiction of women that is so troublesome. It is easy to situate ancient writing within its own historical setting and to realize that much of its expression is historically conditioned and can be reinterpreted for today. Yet the Bible is more than ancient writing. It is cherished as the inspired word of God. As such, many people believe that the historical expression itself is inspired and, therefore, it is meant to be read literally and not changed. Those who promote critical approaches, whether they focus on the author, the text, or the reader, maintain that these issues point out the limitations of an uncritical, literal reading of the Bible.

Deconstruction

Though deconstruction has not been widely accepted by readers of the Bible, it is gaining prominence and should be mentioned here, if only briefly. Deconstruction is a poststructuralist way of thinking that radically challenges the certainty of much modern thought. It insists that the modern tendency of seeking the center or core of reality marginalizes everything that does not conform to that center. Thus the center and the margin are opposite poles of reality, with the center occupying the place of privilege. Deconstruction challenges the privilege of these presumed centers and favors what is marginal. Where structuralism identifies binary opposites (light/darkness, up/down, man/ woman), deconstruction seeks to unmask the hidden powers in such biased oppositions.

Deconstructive critics reject the idea of a world of reality that we seek to discover. They argue that there are only signs that we interpret and thus fashion the worlds that we know. Assumptions about reality may exist, but they are products of our culture; and these assumptions are always undergoing change. This explains the existence of both continuity and discontinuity in culture, in the world of understanding, and in the language we use to represent that world of understanding.

Deconstructive critics also insist that all language is metaphorical, lacking any universally accepted reference. This quality renders language somewhat ambiguous and open to a variety of interpretations. Though meaning is limited by the cultural context, it is possible to image many contexts and, therefore, many possible meanings. Deconstruction challenges the predominant system of interpretation. It is based on the conviction that a text deconstructs itself into various possible meanings. In other words, the text is a representation with no singular meaning.

Strengths and Limitations of Reader-centered Approaches

The most obvious strength of the reader-centered approaches is their attentiveness to the reader. These approaches acknowledge what the author-centered and text-centered criticisms do not, namely, that the reader plays an important role in the construction of meaning. This act of constructing meaning occurs with all reading, whether it focuses on the author, the text, or the reader; but it is only the reader-centered approaches that acknowledge it. Reader-response also brings the message of the passage immediately into the world of the reader, for it is the reader who places it in that world through the very act of reading.

Attention to the pre-understanding of the reader, an aspect of reader-centered approaches, enables the reader to recognize the biases and concerns that are brought to the text. Recognition of these presuppositions prevents the reader from presuming that the author was addressing contemporary concerns, and therefore, was providing answers to those concerns.

An advocacy approach is a form of reader-response that makes explicit the social concerns that the reader brings to the passage. It serves as a lens for reading the biblical text and in this way uncovers themes that might otherwise remain unnoticed. Perhaps the greatest strength of this approach is its potential for transformation of the reader. Since the real goal of reading the Bible is this change, this approach seeks to uncover the religious message of the Bible so that it might enable the reader to work for the elimination of oppressive situations that exist in the world.

Finally, deconstructive approaches remind us that all of our interpretive systems rest on some limited theoretical basis. Since this basis is a human construction, we should be willing to submit it to critical scrutiny lest we think that there is only one way to understand reality, and that way is our own way.

Reader-centered approaches are not without their limitations. Some critics challenge what they call the "affective fallacy." They contend that these approaches confuse the literary work itself with the emotional effect it might have on the reader. Furthermore, they argue that the great diversity of readers who follow these approaches can produce interpretations that are more subjective reading-into-the-text than they are critical reading-what-the-text-says.

Extreme subjectivism is also a danger when one places too much emphasis on the reader's pre-understanding. While recognition of one's presuppositions can help the reader acknowledge biases and inclinations, it can also suggest that any interpretation is a valid interpretation. It is true that advocacy approaches favor the oppressed and marginalized rather than the oppressor or the privileged, but there is a danger that those who practice these approaches will select only those passages that easily lend themselves to this approach. Finally, deconstruction's rejection of any extra-textual reference, whether that be the original religious meaning of the passage or the faith context within which the believing reader interprets the message, undermines the value of the religious tradition.

Summary

The various methods of biblical interpretation can appear to be quite confusing. However, if we remember that there are basically three principal approaches centering on either the author, the text, or the reader, we can see how each method fits into the complicated process of interpretation. The fact that these various methods open up the passage in very different ways need not be reason for concern. This does not mean that we can make the passage mean anything we might want it to mean. It means, instead, that the Bible is a treasury of religious meaning, and the Holy Spirit, working through the very process of interpretation, can open that treasury for our spiritual benefit.

Conclusion

This conclusion is meant to bring the material presented here to some form of closure. The book itself consisted of three parts: 1) a brief account of the history of the ancient world out of which the biblical tradition developed, 2) a synopsis of some of the most important theological themes that constitute that tradition, and 3) a condensed explanation of the various ways of reading the Bible. Some of this material may have seemed quite straightforward; other parts may have appeared to be overly complicated. This is due in part to each reader's degree of familiarity with this material.

A history of the ancient Near Eastern world can be found quite easily. But when reading it, one must remember that there is no such thing as an objective history. Every report is an interpretation of the data, and a history is the interpretation produced by those who have the power to insist that their point of view is the only legitimate point of view. We are all acquainted with the historical account of *How the West Was Won*. However, *How the West Was Lost* may not be as well known, because the losers' side of the story is seldom told.

The stories in the Bible were told from the point of view of believers, first the ancient Israelites and then the early Christians. They are not unbiased stories. They recount how those with faith understood God's action in their lives. The historical dimension of those stories rooted that action in the history of the people. Knowledge of that history throws light on the meaning of the biblical passage.

As important as history may be, the Bible is really a book of theology. It recounts what the people believed; but since their experience of God occurred within their own history, the accounts of that experience and their religious responses to it are clothed in historical garb. Much of the theology that we find in the Bible is historically conditioned. Worship of

God may be a universal human response to divine transcendence, but the way in which this is practiced differs from culture to culture. Believers today may use the psalms of ancient Israel in their worship, but they do not sing them as they sacrifice animals to God. Contemporary people of faith must express that faith in ways that are meaningful today. This is the challenge of interpretation.

What some might consider the easiest aspect of studying the Bible is probably the most daunting, namely, the manner of reading the Bible. Do we read it literally, presuming that there is no difference between ancient perspectives and our own? Or do we take into account cultural differences that we find there? Are we primarily interested in the meaning intended by the original author? And if so, how do we bring that to bear on our own experience? Do we read the Bible as we might read other classical literature, convinced that its religious message will be uncovered in this way? Or is our principal concern with the contemporary reader and the way that reader shapes meaning?

An introduction to the Bible is just that, an introduction. Yet it has sought to uncover just enough of the features of the Bible so that the reader will want to get to know it better. If this happens, the reader will discover that the Bible is an inexhaustible source of challenge and delight, of inspiration and guidance, and a testimony to ultimate meaning and value.

Further Reading

General Introduction

Coogan, Michael D. *The Old Testament: A Historical and Literary Introduction to the Hebrew Scriptures*. New York: Oxford University Press, 2006.

Ehrman, Bart. *The New Testament: A Historical Introduction to the Early Christian Writings*. 4th ed. New York: Oxford University Press, 2007.

Theology

Birch, Bruce C., Walter Brueggemann, Terence E. Fretheim, and David L. Petersen. *A Theological Introduction to the Old Testament*. Nashville, TN: Abingdon, 1999.

Esler, Philip F. *New Testament Theology: Communion and Community*. Minneapolis, MN: Fortress, 2005.

Social World

Matthews, Victor H. *Manners and Customs in the Bible: An Illustrated Guide to Daily Life in Bible Times*. Peabody, MA: Hendrickson, 1988.

Pilch. John J. & Bruce J. Malina, eds. *Handbook of Biblical Social Values*. Peabody, MA: Hendrickson, 1993.

Biblical Interpretation

Harrington, Daniel J. *Interpreting the New Testament*. New Testament Message 1. Wilmington, DE: Michael Glazier, 1979.

Soulen, Richard N., and R. Kendall Soulen. *Handbook of Biblical Criticism*. 3rd ed. Louisville, KY: Westminster John Knox, 2001.

Stuart, Douglas. *Old Testament Exegesis: A Handbook for Students and Pastors*. 3rd ed. Louisville, KY: Westminster John Knox, 2001.

Tate, W. Randolph. *Biblical Interpretation: An Integrated Approach.* Rev. ed. Peabody, MA: Hendrickson, 1997.

Vogels, Walter. *Interpreting the Scripture in the Third Millennium.* Novalis Theological Series. Ottawa, ONT: Novalis, 1993.

Subject Index

Scripture Index